Contents

About this book

Congratulations on your decision to take Edexcel's Foundation Diploma in Society, Health and Development! This book will help you in all eight units of your course, providing opportunities to develop functional skills, Personal, Learning and Thinking Skills, and to learn about the world of work.

There is a chapter devoted to every unit, and each chapter opens with the following:

» Overview – a description of what is covered in the unit

» Skills list – a checklist of the skills covered in the unit

» Job watch – a list of relevant careers

This book contains many features that will help you relate your learning to the workplace and assist you in making links to other parts of the Diploma.

» Margin notes provide interesting facts and get you thinking about the industry.

FIND OUT

Use the glossary in this book, or any other source that you may find helpful (such as the Internet) to find out what the following terms mean: inclusion, discrimination, harassment, prejudice, stereotype, disability, ethnic group, gender, diversity, equality, equality of opportunity, racism, sexism and homophobia.

DID YOU KNOW?

The areas with high rates of 50–69 year olds in employment are Slough, West Berkshire, Buckinghamshire, Rutland, Swindon and Reading.
www.agedscrimination.info

CHECK IT OUT

Immunisation can protect children and adults from certain diseases. For more information, visit www.nhsdirect.nhs.uk and look up the sections about adult and child immunisation.

TRY THIS

Why do you think that people preparing food have to use blue plasters to cover their wounds?

» Activities link directly to Personal, Learning and Thinking Skills and functional skills – all an important part of passing your course and vital for your future career.

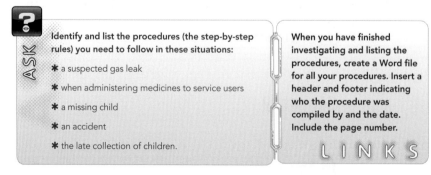

ASK

Identify and list the procedures (the step-by-step rules) you need to follow in these situations:

✳ a suspected gas leak

✳ when administering medicines to service users

✳ a missing child

✳ an accident

✳ the late collection of children.

When you have finished investigating and listing the procedures, create a Word file for all your procedures. Insert a header and footer indicating who the procedure was compiled by and the date. Include the page number.

LINKS

» @work activities help you to think about how your learning could be applied during your work placement.

> » Ask staff how they store confidential records
>
> » Who do they share information with?
>
> » What would they do if someone broke confidentiality and gave information to other people?

» In the Community features provide a snapshot of real issues in the workplace.

» 'I want to be a…' lets you hear from real people what it is like to work in the Society, Health and Development sectors.

Each chapter ends with assessment tips and an opportunity for you to check your skills and summarise what you've learned. You can also find help with technical terms in the glossary on p. 225.

We hope you enjoy using this book, and we wish you the very best for your Diploma course and your future career in Society, Health and Development.

OVERVIEW

This unit has been written to help you learn about the different sectors and organisations that might be involved in working with people in the community. As part of this unit, you will learn how to ask people in the care sectors questions about their work.

People who work in these sectors have a wide range of skills and are employed in a variety of different jobs. However, there are many occasions when they must work together to provide the right type of care for an individual.

Those requiring care will range from children and young people to the elderly, from those needing health and social care, to those in the criminal justice system needing care while they are in custody.

Care workers must ensure that they treat individuals in their care with respect and dignity and that their confidentiality is maintained. When working in the sector, you will learn how to record important details about an individual that can be shared with other care professionals while remaining confidential.

You will also explore the criminal justice system and what happens when people are suspected of breaking the law. Laws are made by Parliament and then enforced by the police, but other organisations in the sector also work with the police to try and reduce crime.

The police often have to work with the fire and ambulance services when attending the scene of an accident or major incident, when the work that they do together can help save lives.

By the time you've finished this chapter, you will have a good understanding of the many different organisations that work with people in the community.

Exploring the Sectors

01

You will need this knowledge if you are considering a career as a:

» doctor
» midwife
» nurse
» health visitor
» early years practitioner
» care worker
» probation officer
» teacher
» youth worker
» psychologist
» childminder
» after school worker
» play worker
» play therapist
» social worker
» police officer
» substance misuse worker
» psychiatrist
» ambulance care assistant
» renal technician
» dietician
» art therapist.

Skills list

On completion of this unit, you will:

» be able to identify questions to investigate the sectors

» know the purpose of and structure within and across the sectors

» understand the range of services delivered in the sectors

» know the roles of organisations and how they work together to deliver services in a community.

Being able to identify questions to help you investigate the sectors

FIGURE 1.1 Libraries are just one source of information

Learning to learn

It is important when you begin to study any subject that you understand how to access information. Information can be gathered from a variety of sources. It is important to gather information from a variety of sources because people will have different views.

Listening

Much of what you learn will be learnt from the teacher in your class and from talking to other people and staff in different organisations.

You will need to make sure that you are *ready to listen*. You can do this in the following ways.

» Try to prepare beforehand – read books, magazines and notes on the subject.

» Make sure you are comfortable.

» Do not get distracted by your fellow learners (try to block out any distractions such as noise).

» Listen with an open mind (do not prejudge or begin with a fixed idea).

» Check your attitude (be eager to learn).

» Focus on what the teacher (or other person) is really saying.

» Try to think of questions that you can ask at the end.

» Ask questions and ask for clarification on any areas of the discussion that you did not understand.

Note taking

It is important when you are listening to your teacher that you take notes. You will need this information for your assignments at the end of each unit. You will need to:

» look at your notes from the previous session

» make sure you come prepared with paper and pens

» focus on what the teacher (or other person) is saying

» write quickly so that you get as much information down as possible

» try to get the key terms and meanings – do not try to write everything down

» try to develop your own form of shorthand. Do not worry about spellings or presentation – your notes are for your use only and as long as you can read them the presentation does not matter

» underline key terms

» write a question mark next to your notes if you do not understand something – and ask your teacher later for an explanation

» check with other learners to make sure you have not left anything out

» rewrite your notes when you get home (this will help you to remember the session and reinforce your learning)

» expand and develop your notes using books and other sources of information.

ASK

Listen to the news on the television or radio and make notes on the information given. Aim to write as little as possible but make sure you get the key points

Team work

It is important that you work as part of a team. It stands to reason that if you have more people you will get more work done and have more information to work from. You can work as part of a team to:

» gather and share information from the library

» give joint presentations to the rest of the group

» complete an assignment – with each member of the group having responsibility for a different piece of information

» form study groups and test each other on your knowledge.

FIGURE 1.2 **Radios help police teamwork**

TEAMWORK

Work in a team of four people and investigate the community justice sector. Allocate one of the following topics to each person so that you cover all the knowledge needed. Put your work together and prepare a presentation. Present your findings to the rest of the group.

The structure of the justice sector

The purpose of the justice sector

The range of services available in the justice sector

The roles of individuals and how they work with others

How to do research

Throughout your studies you will be required to carry out research. This means that you will be given a topic and you will need to gather information about it. When doing research, it is important:

» to identify the topic (what you will be investigating)

» to identify key questions or areas that you need to research – in this unit the key questions that you need to ask are:

– What are the structures of the different sectors?

– What are their purposes?

– What range of services do they provide?

– What are the roles (the jobs that people do) in the organisation?

– How do the different organisations work together?

» to brainstorm (jot down in no particular order all the things you think you will need to know or already know)

» to search the web (Internet) for information

» to go to the library and look at books on the subject

» to watch any television programmes on your subject and take notes

» to take notes in class

» to talk to people who work in the sector

» to write down your findings and divide your research into sections with clear headings – otherwise it will become too big and unmanageable.

Using the Internet

The Internet is a good source of information. You can get information about a topic quickly using the Internet. You will need to use a search engine such as:

» www.google.com

» www.askjeeves.com

Type in the key words of the subject that you want to research and Google (or whichever search engine you use) will list the different sites that match your key words. Remember that you will need to decide how best to use the information found on a website, and whether it is to be trusted.

Using books and the library

Books are a good source of information. Libraries usually organise their books under subject headings and numbers – for example, books on social work may be in the 'Sociology' section, numbered from 601.00 onwards. Books in this area of study may be difficult to find because they will come under a variety of subject headings, such as Health, Education, Psychology, Sociology. Talk to the librarian who will help you find the relevant sections.

It is important that you take notes from the books you read and that you remember to make *reference* to (identify) where you got your information from. Your list of references is normally called a *bibliography*. You will need to include a note of:

» who wrote the book (the author)

» what the book was called (the title)

» when the book was published (the year)

» who published the book (the publisher)

» the page number where you got your information.

For example if you used this book you would need to state:

Eden, S. (author)

Society, Health and Development (title)

2008 (year of publication)

Pearson Education (publisher)

p. 2 (where you got your information)

TEAMWORK

In groups of three, visit the library and find out as much information as you can about:

✱ the different health services available for the elderly

✱ the care available for victims or witnesses of crime.

Make a list of all the books you used and prepare a bibliography for other people to see. You will need to include a list of at least six books.

Knowing the purposes of the sectors, and the structures within and across them

Social care sector

The social care sector is huge and can be confusing. However, its main purpose is to provide care for those who are in need. This covers issues relating to all age groups and to all ethnic groups. The Department of Health (which is part of the government) sets the standards for the sector. The Department of Health monitors and sets the rules for all parts of the sector, even private organisations. The Department of Health also controls the NHS (National Health Service).

FIGURE 1.3 **Meals on wheels provide support in the community**

There are different types of organisations that provide social care services.

Statutory

Statutory provision is what the government provides. It is paid for by the government out of the taxes people pay. It includes services such as social workers, housing, and day centres. Although some of these services are provided directly by the government, others are provided by private companies.

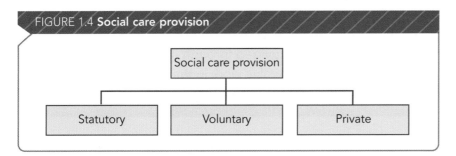

FIGURE 1.4 **Social care provision**

Voluntary

Voluntary organisations are national or local organisations that have been set up by people to meet the needs of certain groups. They may get money from the government, they may fund raise for themselves, or people may volunteer their services for free.

Voluntary organisations normally get set up because of a lack of government provision. They include organisations such as the NSPCC, Home-Start and MIND. Some voluntary organisations help young people with issues such as pregnancy, and drug and substance misuse.

Using the Internet, look at one voluntary organisation such as the NSPCC, Home-Start or MIND

Produce a list of six bullet points identifying what your chosen organisation does.

Private

Private provision is completely paid for by the service user (the person needing the service). For example, lots of families in today's society pay for private residential homes for the elderly.

Using the Internet, books, newspapers and local leaflets, find information about one statutory and one private organisation in your area.

Identify what these organisations do and how they try to help people.

Discuss your findings with the rest of the group.

Health sector

The main purpose of the health sector is to take care of, promote and meet the health needs of people in Britain. Like social care, health services are also provided through different agencies (organisations) and also involve work in the community.

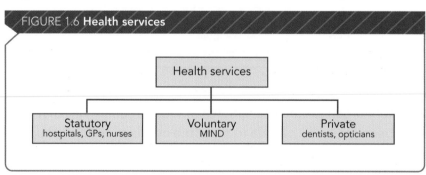

FIGURE 1.6 **Health services**

Health services

Statutory hostpitals, GPs, nurses	Voluntary MIND	Private dentists, opticians

FIGURE 1.5
Ambulance services are part of statutory health provision

Department of Health

The Department of Health's overall purpose is to help improve the health and wellbeing of everyone in England. It does this by:

» setting overall standards of health care and passing these on to other organisations

» checking that public money is spent correctly

» checking and inspecting the standard and safety of health and social care services.

FIGURE 1.7 Management of Health Services in England

The Department of Health
sets overall standards of health care and passes these on to

The NHS
which is responsible for all National Health Services in England and Wales. The NHS passes these on to

Strategic health authorities (in local areas)
which are responsible for managing services locally.
The strategic health authorities pass these on to

Different trusts
to ensure that services are provided in key areas – these
include acute trusts, ambulance trusts, mental health trusts,
and primary care trusts which provide services such as GPs

Children and young people

New laws have been introduced to ensure that children are taken care of properly. There have been cases in the past where children have died because people in different sectors were unsure who was responsible for the child.

The Children Act 2004 introduced a Children's Commissioner who has responsibility for children and young people.

The law insists that each local authority has a Director of Children's Services who is responsible for education and social services when the case involves a child or young person.

Because children and young people come under lots of different sectors, the government has introduced **children's trusts** at a local level. Children's trusts bring together professionals from different sectors so that all the needs of children can be met.

Justice

The main purpose of the justice system is:

» to defend people

» to protect the innocent

» to punish the guilty.

The justice system is concerned with protecting people by catching offenders, taking them to court and punishing them if they are found guilty.

Parliament

Parliament is responsible for making UK law. Parliament is made up of three parts: the House of Commons, the House of Lords, and the Crown.

What does Parliament do?
Parliament is responsible for:

» making laws

» controlling finance (the House of Commons has to approve proposals for government taxes and expenditure)

» protecting the interests of the public by acting as a check on the government's work (for example, making the government defend their policies and explain them to the public).

The government has overall responsibility for justice. The department responsible for justice is called the Ministry of Justice. It is led by the Secretary of State for Justice. The Ministry of Justice is responsible for:

» criminal law

» civil law

» the courts

» family and administrative justice systems

» tribunals

» legal aid

» prisons

» the probation service.

Police

The Home Office is responsible for immigration and the police.

When members of the public are involved in dealing with the legal system, the following Acts of Parliament are the most relevant:

» Police and Criminal Evidence Act 1994

» Human Rights Act 1998

» Crime and Disorder Act 1998

» Police Reform Act 2002

» Criminal Justice Act 2003.

Using the Internet, find out who currently holds the following jobs in Britain:

Prime Minister   Minister for Education

Deputy Prime Minister   Secretary of State for Justice

Minister for Health

With another learner, choose one of the following roles:

* dietician

* probation officer

* mental health nurse

* care worker in the community

* play worker

* early years worker.

Try to identify what sector they work in and what work they do on a day to day basis. Look at magazines and job adverts – try to find out how much they get paid, how many hours they work each week and what qualifications they need.

When you have found out this information prepare a presentation for the rest of the group, and present your findings.

When you have heard about all the job roles from the other learners identify what job you would like to do in the future and why.

LINKS

@work

» Ask staff what other organisations they work with – do they ever have to deal with other professionals such as the police, doctors, teachers?

» Ask how they communicate with other sectors – do they talk on the telephone, do they send letters, do they have meetings, do they use e-mail?

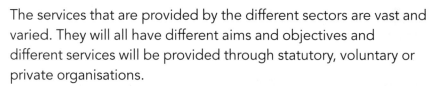

Understanding the range of services delivered in the sectors

Range of services

The services that are provided by the different sectors are vast and varied. They will all have different aims and objectives and different services will be provided through statutory, voluntary or private organisations.

FIGURE 1.8 **Reading with an elderly man suffering from dementia**

TABLE 1.1 The range of services provided			
Health	**Social care**	**Children and young people**	**Justice**
Hospitals – health care	Social workers	Schools	Police
Private hospitals	Carers	Nurseries	Neighbourhood Watch
Ambulances – transport to hospital	Meals on wheels	After school clubs	Probation services
Dieticians – help with healthy eating and specialist diets	Dieticians	Adventure playgrounds	Courts
	Home helps	Extended schools	Family courts
GPs	Substance misuse advisers	Childminding	Victim support services
Hospital doctors	Mental health teams	Colleges	Prisons
Consultants	Housing services	Private schools	Young offender institutions
Midwives	Counselling services	Boarding schools	Domestic violence units
Nurses	Respite care	Residential care	Child protection units
Health visitors	Day centres	Homeless advice and support	Citizens Advice services
Psychologists	Residential care	Connexions	
Therapists	Supported housing	Sure Start	
Opticians	Bereavement advice and support	NSPCC	
Dentists	Advice and support for the homeless	ChildLine	
Clinics – sexual health advice	Rehabilitation teams	Foster care	
Speech and language therapists	Domiciliary care	Respite care	
Paramedics	Learning disability units	Outreach workers	
Chiropodists	Advice and information services	YMCA	
NHS Direct –telephone service	AA (Alcoholics Anonymous)	Advice and information services	
	Women's aid	Adoption services	

Look at the range of services available in the different sectors in the chart above. With another learner identify the services that are private, statutory and voluntary. Look at the services available in your local area. Can you add more services to the list?

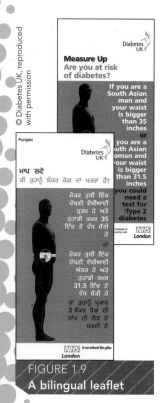

FIGURE 1.9
A bilingual leaflet

Choose one of the sectors from the chart on the previous page and produce a text message that could be sent to service users identifying what services are available to them in their local area. To make sure your message is clear, send your text message to other learners in the group.

With the rest of the group, discuss the range of local services available and the benefits to service users.

@work

» Look to see if there are leaflets on the services that are provided. Collect them for future information.

» Are there leaflets in different languages?

Knowing the roles of the organisations and how they work together to deliver services in the community

Social care

Care homes – care homes are available for those who need medical care or just looking after. They can be provided by the state or they can be private. Care homes provide residential care mainly for the elderly, people with disabilities and children who have been placed in residential care.

Care in your own home – local authorities send care workers into people's homes, either directly or through an agency. Carers will help with preparing meals, bathing, shopping, and cleaning. The length of time the carer will spend will vary, depending on the level of need – it may be an hour a day or 24 hours. Local councils will also provide grants for adaptations to people's homes – for example, to fit a shower.

Direct payment schemes – this is a new initiative by the government. Service users are given money directly so that they can buy their own care. This gives them more choice over who cares for them and when.

Nursing agencies – nursing agencies send nurses to people's homes when they need nursing care. This service is normally provided after someone leaves hospital.

General Social Care Council – the General Social Care Council regulates and sets the standards for the social care workforce.

Skills for Care and Development – this is the Sector Skills Council for social care, children and young people's workforces in the UK. It represents the viewpoints of the social care workforce. It decides what qualifications are needed for work in the sector.

Commission for Social Care Inspection (CSCI) – the CSCI registers and inspects social care services in England.

Social Care Institute of Excellence – this organisation develops knowledge about good practice in the sector.

Substance misuse advice – a large number of local authorities have organisations that provide advice, guidance and support for those who are dependent on drugs and alcohol. They employ trained counsellors and help people with housing, seeking benefits and getting back to work. Their aim is to help people stop using addictive substances such as drugs and alcohol.

Social workers – social workers are concerned with the welfare of vulnerable children, young people and adults. They provide and organise a variety of services for those who are at most risk.

Respite care – respite care is available to help carers who need a break. Parents or carers who look after children or adults with disabilities or mental health problems can use this service. They are able to leave the child or adult with a registered respite carer for a short time. This can be for a few hours or longer, depending on need.

Day centres – day centres provide specialist services for different groups of people – for example, elderly people, homeless people, people from different ethnic groups, and people with disabilities. Day centres may provide a drop-in service so that people can get a hot meal, socialise with others and get advice and guidance.

Supported housing – some elderly people and people with disabilities need supported housing. They do not need to be cared for totally but they need support to be there if they need it. Some elderly people do not want to go into residential care but they do need someone available to check that they are all right. Supported housing allows for independent living – a manager or warden will live on the premises or nearby and provide support if requested. Support could include help with cooking or shopping, or just checking that the person feels safe.

Advice and information services – all local authorities provide services for advice and guidance. People in the local community will be able to gain information about services through the Internet, by telephone or from leaflets.

Phone up your local authority and ask them to provide you with information about adult social care in your local area. Identify whether the service was useful. Were they helpful? Was it easy to get the information you wanted?

Health

Doctors, nurses, midwives and dentists all have to register with a professional body once they have finished their studies. They cannot work in the UK unless they register.

General Medical Council (GMC) – the GMC regulates the medical profession. Doctors have to be registered with the GMC to practise medicine in the UK. Doctors who do not act professionally will be called before the Council and they can be struck off the register.

General Dental Council – regulates the dental profession in the UK. Dentists have to register with this body.

Nursing and Midwifery Council – this organisation registers nurses and midwives.

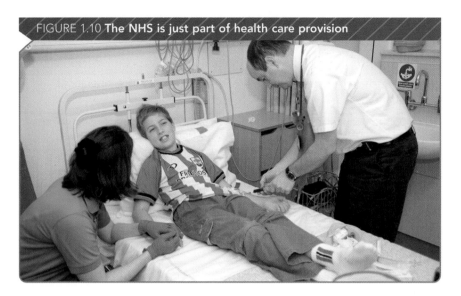

FIGURE 1.10 The NHS is just part of health care provision

National Health Service (NHS) – the NHS is responsible for all health services in England and Wales.

Strategic health authorities – there are 10 strategic health authorities in Britain which are responsible for health in local areas. They develop, plan and make sure their local NHS organisations perform well. They set up trusts in local areas to ensure that services are provided.

Acute trusts – make sure that hospitals provide high quality services. They are responsible for improving hospitals in the local area.

Ambulance trusts – provide emergency access to health care. They provide ambulances to get people to hospital urgently.

Mental health trusts – provide services locally for those who have mental health problems. They provide care in the community through counselling and nursing.

Primary care trusts – provide 'first contact' health care for local people – for example, GP services, health visitors, chiropodists and dentists.

Secondary health care – this refers to health care services that are provided by hospitals or other centres for people who need further care after going to their GP.

Skills for Health – this is the Sector Skills Council for the health workforce in the UK. It represents the viewpoints of the health care workforce. It decides what qualifications are needed to work in the sector.

TABLE 1.2 Roles and responsibilities of organisations in the health sector

Organisation	Roles and Responsibilities
Hospitals	Health facilities for the local community. May include emergency care, operations, advice and guidance
Ambulances	Provide transport to hospital in an emergency. Ambulance crews (paramedics) will also provide emergency care – for example, at the scene of an accident
Dieticians	Provide advice on healthy eating and specialist diets for people with food allergies, diabetes, obesity
GPs	First point of contact for those who are unwell. Responsible for diagnosing illnesses and other conditions. They refer people to specialists if they need additional services
Consultants	Specialists in a particular health field – for example, a specialist in children's health, an ear specialist, a heart specialist, a bone specialist
Midwives	Look after women when they give birth
Health visitors	Normally based in the local community. They support, monitor and advise women with young babies, and work with people who suffer from chronic illnesses or have disabilities
Opticians	Responsible for general eye care. Opticians check people's sight and the health of their eyes, and prescribe glasses if needed
Dentists	Responsible for the health and care of people's teeth
Chiropodists	Look after the health needs of people's feet
NHS Direct	A 24-hour telephone service which people can ring for information and advice on health issues

ASK

With a friend, find out what the following specialists are called (for example, a person who operates on bones is called an orthopaedic surgeon).

A doctor who specialises in the care of children.

A doctor who specialises in the care of elderly people.

A doctor who specialises in the care of pregnant women.

Children and young people

Services for children and young people fall under all the different sectors. For example, children and young people may use services such as hospitals, GPs, police, and social services. It is hard to look at services for children separately. However, some services are provided just for children and their families.

CWDC – this is the Sector Skills Council for the children's workforce in the UK. It represents the viewpoints of the child care workforce. It decides what qualifications are needed for work in the sector.

ASK

With another learner in the group find out what CWDC stands for. Using the Internet find out their aims and objectives and what they do as an organisation.

Ofsted – Ofsted is the Office for Standards in Education, Children's Services and Skills. It is responsible for checking and inspecting organisations such as schools and nurseries to make sure they are operating to the required standards.

TABLE 1.3 **Roles and responsibilities of organisations in the children's service sector**

Organisation	Roles and responsibilities
Schools	Responsible for the education of children from the age of 5–16 years
Nurseries/playgroups/ day centres	Provide care and education for children aged 0–5 years
After school clubs	Provide play facilities for children after they finish school. They also provide facilities and activities during the school holidays
Extended schools	Provide a range of services on school premises such as parenting classes, after school clubs, health visitors, therapy, help getting back to work
Childminders	Look after other people's children, usually in their own home. This can be for a few hours a day or all day. The level of provision is decided between the childminder and the parent or guardian
Colleges	Provide education for young people once they have left school
ChildLine	Provides a telephone advice service for children and young people who may be experiencing difficulties such as abuse. Children can telephone ChildLine and discuss their problems with a trained counsellor. They will be given advice and guidance
Foster care services	Foster care is arranged by social services. It is a facility for children who may be finding it difficult to be cared for at home for a variety of reasons. Children can be looked after by foster parents for a short or long time. The length of stay is dependent on need

Justice

Your Local Criminal Justice Board is responsible for reducing crime and administering justice in your local area. It is responsible for:

» improving the delivery of justice (making it more efficient so that we feel safer)

» improving the service provided to victims and witnesses

» securing public confidence (making sure we all think the justice service is doing its job).

Skills for Justice – this is the Sector Skills Council for those who work in the UK justice sector. It includes the majority of the uniformed services. It is responsible for deciding what qualifications are needed for work in the sector.

FIGURE 1.11 **Justice Sector**

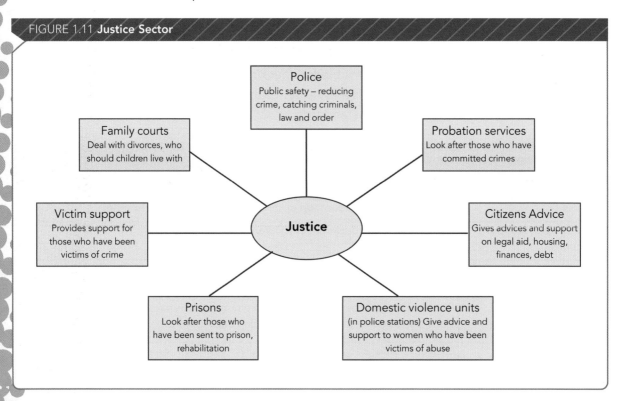

Police
Public safety – reducing crime, catching criminals, law and order

Family courts
Deal with divorces, who should children live with

Probation services
Look after those who have committed crimes

Victim support
Provides support for those who have been victims of crime

Justice

Citizens Advice
Gives advices and support on legal aid, housing, finances, debt

Prisons
Look after those who have been sent to prison, rehabilitation

Domestic violence units
(in police stations) Give advice and support to women who have been victims of abuse

ASK

Choose an organisation from one of the above sectors. Using the Internet as a means of research, produce an information sheet which tells other learners:

✱ the aims and objectives of the organisation you have chosen

✱ who they provide services for

✱ what they do on a daily basis

✱ what types of professionals they have working for them.

When you have done this, prepare a presentation for the rest of the group. Use your information sheet as a handout.

I want to be...

... a health care assistant in the community

Name: Anne Kelly

Age: 28 years

Salary: £20,000 per annum (per year)

Employer: Local GP – primary care team

Hours of work: 35 hours per week (7 hours per day)

» **Roles and responsibilities (what I do in my job as a health care assistant in the community):**

- I go into the office first and check if I have any messages or e-mails or any urgent visits to make
- I check my diary and the people I need to see that day
- I normally visit on average six people per day
- I visit people with a range of health care needs – such as those with learning disabilities, the elderly, people with Alzheimer's
- I change dressings
- I check blood pressure
- I check glucose levels
- I record and document the condition of the patients
- I liaise with the service user's carer
- I work as part of a team and have to attend team meetings weekly

» **Qualifications:**

NVQ Level 3 Health and Social Care Clean driving licence

» **What I like about my job:**

Every day is different. I like being out and about and looking after a variety of service users. I like the variety in my job. I would find it hard to be in an office. I like mixing with the local community.

» **The hardest part of my job:**

I work in a rural area and the travelling can sometimes be difficult. The service users can live as far as 10 miles away. Driving is an essential skill when you work in a rural community. You could not do the job if you did not have a car.

✳ Anne Kelly

In the Community

Mobility issues →

Martin is 72 years of age. He lives on his own in a two-bedroom house. He does not have any immediate family.

Martin has arthritis and finds it difficult to get about. He uses a stick to help him balance. He cannot get up and down the stairs and so he has moved his bed to the front room. Just recently Martin has discovered that he has diabetes and that he must control and monitor what he eats.

Martin is finding it difficult to sleep at night because the teenagers who live next door get drunk and play loud music. Martin has tried to talk to them but they laugh and throw stones at him. They have broken his fence and thrown things at his window.

Martin is feeling very anxious about the situation and worries about having to go outside to do his food shopping. The local corner shop recently closed and the nearest supermarket is a 15-minute walk away.

Questions

1. Make a list of all the professionals Martin might come across.

2. What help may Martin need?

3. List one statutory, one voluntary and one private service that could help Martin. Explain what help they could provide.

4. Make a list of the advantages of being cared for in your own home.

5. Make a list of the advantages of being cared for in a residential care home.

6. Which type of care would you prefer?

Assessment Tips

To pass your assessment for this unit you will need to consider carefully all the information in this chapter and all the information that has been given to you by your teacher.

To show that you are developing as a competent researcher and learner, you will need to record your actions – and your contributions in any group work.

Any presentations you do should include visual aids, such as charts and diagrams, and you should be able to fully explain their use. Following your presentation, it is useful to evaluate: decide what went well and what didn't go quite so well. Was your research thorough or were there areas you could have looked at in more depth? What would you do differently if you had to give this presentation again? How could it be improved?

The efforts you make show that you are developing personal learning and thinking skills. You will be given credit for this and also for showing evidence of your functional skills.

FIND OUT

>> You will need to research into the different sectors and their purposes. You will need to look at how to do research to meet this criterion. You will need to identify the stages of research you went through – for example, brainstorming, making notes, identifying questions, going to the library. You will need to identify and include the questions you used. You will also need to make a list of any problems you may have had and how you overcame these.

>> You will need to find out about the overall structure and purpose of the social care sector, health sector, children and young people sector, and justice sector. You could present this part of your assignment in the form of a diagram. Try using the Internet to find out this information.

>> For this part of your assignment you will need to find out how the sectors work together to provide two different services – for example, if a child was being physically abused a doctor would examine them, a police officer would investigate the offence, social services might place the child with a foster carer, and all the sectors would be represented on the local safeguarding children's board.

>> You will need to find out about four organisations that work together in your local area to deliver a service and/or improve the community. You will need to find out about the role of each of the four organisations. Try to get leaflets about organisations in your local area to help you with this.

SUMMARY / SKILLS CHECK

» The different sectors

✔ **Care** – The social care sector's main purpose is to provide care for those that are in need.

✔ **Health** – The main aims (purpose) of the health sector is to promote and meet the health needs of people in Britain.

✔ **Children and young people** – Children and young people receive care from many different sectors. Therefore, the Government has introduced the local level service Children's Trust to bring together different professionals from the different sectors to meet children's needs.

✔ **Justice** – The purposes of the justice system are to defend people, protect the innocent and punish/rehabilitate the guilty.

» Range of services delivered in the sectors

✔ The services provided by the different sectors are vast and varied. Different services will be provided by statutory, voluntary or private organisations. These organisations have different aims and objectives.

✔ **Social care services include**: carers, Meals on Wheels, dieticians, help with independent living, substance misuse advice, mental health teams, social workers, housing services, adult social care, immigration services, counsellors, support for ex-offenders.

✔ **Health care services include**: hospitals – NHS and private, ambulances – transport to hospital, dieticians – help with healthy eating and specialist diets, GPs, dentists, chiropodists, health visitors.

✔ **Children and young people's services include**: childminders, nurseries, schools – state-run and private (including boarding schools), after school clubs and extended schools, colleges, adventure playgrounds, residential care, Connexions.

✔ **Justice services include**: the police force, Neighbourhood Watch, probation services, criminal justice, magistrates and family courts, victim support services, the prison service and young offender institutions, domestic violence units.

OVERVIEW

In any care setting it is generally believed that all people should be treated as individuals, with dignity and respect. This unit is concerned with the beliefs, principles and values of the different sectors explored in Unit 1.

Everyone has ideas about what they think is right and wrong, but it is important that when we work with other people we work to the same values and principles. It is important that we understand what is meant by dignity and respect and understand how we can observe these principles in a work setting.

One way of exploring your own attitudes, principles and values is through a case study, and acting out the roles of the people involved – whether this is the role of the care professional involved or of the individual requiring care and support in a given situation. This will help you to apply the appropriate principles and values in your practice in a care setting.

You will need to consider how the different sectors promote the rights of individuals in their care and whether those individuals have equality of opportunity in expressing their own principles and values.

Throughout this unit you will explore concepts such as discrimination, harassment, racism, prejudice, stereotype, disability, inclusion, ethnicity, gender, diversity, sexism and equality. You need to understand what these terms mean and also reflect on your ideas and attitudes.

You should remember to treat people as you would want to be treated in similar circumstances.

02

Exploring Principles and Values

Skills list

On completion of this unit, you will:

» Understand what is meant by rights, responsibilities, equality and diversity and why they are important when working with individuals, groups and communities

» Understand what is meant by confidentiality, why it is important and the possible consequences of a breach of confidentiality

» Know the purpose and impact of key legislation and codes of practice that relate to principles and values

» Know how different values might be supported in a variety of settings within the sectors

» Be able to reflect on own principles and values in relation to the work of the sectors.

Job watch

You will need this knowledge if you are considering any career in health and social care, including all of the following job roles:

» doctor
» midwife
» nurse
» health visitor
» early years practitioner
» care worker
» probation officer
» youth worker
» childminder
» social worker
» police officer.

Understanding what is meant by rights, responsibilities, equality and diversity and why they are important

Rights

It is important to understand that people in the UK have rights and responsibilities to and for each other and their communities. Rules and laws are needed to ensure that all people in society are protected. On the whole most people believe that individuals have the right to:

- a good education
- be healthy
- vote
- freedom of expression
- a fair trial
- marry
- respect for private and family life
- freedom from harm and torture
- protection from discrimination
- privacy
- confidentiality.

THINK

Discuss with other learners what additional rights should be given to people.

Do young people have the same rights as adults?

Discuss whether children should be given more rights.

Responsibilities

With rights come responsibilities. A responsible person:

- accepts that people are different
- treats all people with respect
- cares about other people's feelings
- seeks other people's viewpoints

» takes care of people in the community

» looks after their environment

» does not discriminate against other individuals

» does not cause a nuisance to others

» does not damage other people's property

» does not break the law.

FIND OUT

Use the glossary in this book, or any other source that you may find helpful (such as the Internet) to find out what the following terms mean: inclusion, discrimination, harassment, prejudice, stereotype, disability, ethnic group, gender, diversity, equality, equality of opportunity, racism, sexism and homophobia.

TEAMWORK

Spend 15 minutes as a group discussing what you think is meant by 'rights' and 'responsibilities'.

After this discussion you should be able to:

✱ explain what you mean by rights

✱ explain what you mean by responsibilities.

People who may be discriminated against

Most people, at some point in their life, have experienced discrimination. This may have been based on their gender or their age, or it may just have been a case of people making assumptions about them without knowing them. However, certain people in society are more likely to be discriminated against than others.

REFLECT

Think back to a time when you have been discriminated against:

✱ How did you feel?

✱ How did you react?

✱ What did you do?

✱ How would you have liked to be treated?

Discuss your views with another learner. Identify why it is important to treat people fairly.

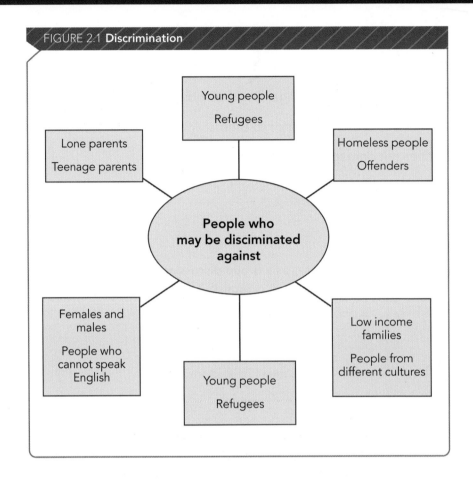

FIGURE 2.1 **Discrimination**

Young people
Refugees

Lone parents
Teenage parents

Homeless people
Offenders

People who may be discriminated against

Females and males
People who cannot speak English

Young people
Refugees

Low income families
People from different cultures

Effects of discrimination

Discrimination is exceptionally damaging. It can affect people in both the short term and the long term. It is important to remember that people will react differently to discrimination. People may react in a variety of ways. They may become anxious, depressed or withdrawn. Or they may feel angry and become aggressive. They may lose feel worthless and disillusioned and that they are losing their identity as an individual.

As a result of such feelings the individual is likely to have low confidence and low self-esteem. They may lack motivation and fail to achieve at school, college, university or at work. Or they may suffer from mental health problems or become involved in substance misuse or criminal activity. These individuals may be socially excluded and fail to achieve their full potential.

The importance of treating people equally and fairly

It is important to remember that everyone is different. We should never make assumptions about anybody. We should always ask people about themselves and what is important to them. We must treat people fairly because people have rights in law and we can be punished if we break the law. However, we also have a moral obligation as a responsible citizen.

If we treat people with dignity and respect, they will feel good about themselves – valued and respected. This gives them the opportunity to achieve their full potential in life. Individuals who are empowered can learn from each other – maybe learning a new language or about a different culture – creating greater tolerance. In turn, people will care for each other and work together to benefit the community.

TEAMWORK

In groups of three, carry out a mini-survey in your school. Talk to other learners and find out their ethnic background. Identify how many different groups of people you have in your school. Ask other learners if they have ever been discriminated against, and how they felt.

Discuss your findings with the rest of the group.

LINKS

Present your findings in the form of a bar chart (see example below).

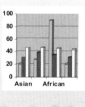

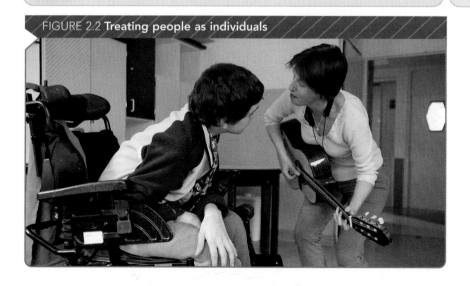

FIGURE 2.2 **Treating people as individuals**

@work

» Observe staff in your work placement setting. How do they make people from different backgrounds feel comfortable?

» Ask how they would deal with someone who was racist or sexist.

» Are there staff from a variety of backgrounds (for example, Asian, African, Afro-Caribbean, other European countries)?

» How many male workers are there, and how many female?

Understanding what is meant by confidentiality, why it is important and the possible consequences of a breach of confidentiality

Confidentiality

Confidentiality is the term used to refer to the safekeeping and protection of information about people we come into contact with in health and social care settings.

FIGURE 2.3 **Confidentiality includes storing files securely**

It refers to the procedures (rules) we must follow when service users themselves or others tell us things.

This section looks at how we manage information and who we can pass it on to.

TEAMWORK

In groups of three, discuss what is meant by the term gossiping.

In your discussions, you should:

* talk about the impact that gossiping may have on people's lives

* identify how people may feel if they are the subject of gossip

* identify any damage that you think can be caused by gossip.

Data Protection Act 1998

When we work in the health and social care sector we are exposed to and come into contact with lots of information about clients and service users. Staff will have access to very personal information about people. Individuals have a right to be protected and personal details should be kept secret from the rest of the world. Only certain people should have access to information.

The Data Protection Act 1998 is the law that governs how we should behave in relation to information about others. The Data Protection Act states that information must be fairly and lawfully processed, for limited purposes only. Stored information should be adequate for the purpose intended but not excessive. It should be accurate, only shared with authorised personnel, kept securely and for no longer than is necessary for the purpose.

JOIN IN

In groups of three, make a list of the information you would keep about service users, and information that does not need to be recorded (see example opposite).

Give reasons for your answer.

Information that needs to be recorded	Information that should not be recorded
Name Address	Number of boyfriends the client has had

Policies and procedures

In all settings in health and social care there must be a confidentiality policy and procedures for dealing with and storing information. This policy will tell staff:

» how information should be recorded

» how information should be stored

» who is responsible for making decisions about the information held

» what to do in an emergency

» what information must be passed on (for example, if a child tells you that they have been abused).

Consequences of breaking confidentiality

If you reveal personal information about service users without their consent, it is unlikely that they will trust you in the future. They will lose confidence in you and stop telling you things that may be important to their care and support.

Almost certainly they will feel angry and, depending on the nature of the confidence, they may feel embarrassed. You will have invaded their privacy and undermined their rights. They may feel unimportant and undervalued as an individual.

Also, when confidentiality is broken, the service user's safety may be put at risk. The information may be misused for criminal purposes, for identity theft, property theft or extortion. In serious cases, you could be taken to court for breaking the law

FIGURE 2.4 **Conversations should be confidential**

TEAMWORK

In pairs, make a list of all the different types of records that may be kept on adults and children (charts, observations, etc.).

Identify who may need to see different types of information about service users. For example, a doctor may need to see the health observations that you have made, a dietician may need to see what the person likes to eat, or when an individual is in custodial care, a police officer may need to know if they have any health issues, such as asthma or diabetes.

Discuss why it is important that records are factual and correct. What are the consequences of recording things wrongly?

LINKS

» Ask staff how they store confidential records

» Who do they share information with?

» What would they do if someone broke confidentiality and gave information to other people?

Knowing the purpose and impact of key legislation and codes of practice that relate to principles and values

Understanding the law

Human Rights Act 1998

This states the basis human rights to which all individuals are entitled.

Sex Discrimination Act 1975

This states that you are not allowed to discriminate on the grounds of sex in areas such as employment, education, housing, and provision of goods and services.

Race (Amendment) Act 2000

This states that you are not allowed to discriminate on the grounds of race in areas such as employment, education, housing, and provision of goods and services.

Care Standards Act 2000

The Care Standards Act ensures that all those who look after others are registered and conform to good practice.

TEAMWORK

Divide into two groups.

Group 1 should use the Internet to find information about the Human Rights Act 1998. Group 2 should use the Internet to find information about the Care Standards Act 2000.

Hint: you can find these acts on the Office of Public Sector information website, www.opsi.gov.uk. Click on the site map and scroll down to 'Legislation', and then click on 'Acts'. This will take you to a calendar of year dates, you then click on the year in which the Act was passed and scroll down the alphabetical list until you reach the Act you want to find out about.

Once you have found the Act you are researching, you should:

✱ list the rights to which people are entitled (Group 1)

✱ list the standards that care professionals should follow when caring for individuals (Group 2).

Children Act 2004

This is concerned with the principles of the government programme **Every Child Matters**. The Children Act 2004 introduced the following requirements:

» closer working between different professionals who come into contact with children

» the wishes of children must be taken into account

» better sharing of information between organisations

» a Children's Commissioner for England

» Local Safeguarding Children Boards to help protect children at risk from abuse

» a duty for local authorities to promote the education of children in care.

Care Homes for Older People: National Minimum Standards – Care Home Regulations 2003

This is concerned with the standards people must meet when caring for the elderly. It looks at:

» health and personal care

» social activities

» complaints

» protection of vulnerable people

» staffing

» suitable environments

» management

» records and record keeping.

Disability Discrimination Act 2005

This looks at the experiences of those who have special needs (disabilities). Staff and settings have to make adjustments to the environment and facilities so that people with disabilities can attend.

Mental Capacity Act 2005

This protects people who have mental health problems. It looks at who can make decisions for those who are unable to do so.

Age Discrimination Act 2006

This makes it wrong to discriminate against a person because of their age. It relates to employment. You are not allowed to discriminate when you are recruiting people, promoting people or providing training for people.

FIGURE 2.5 **Skills are for life**

UN (United Nations) Convention on the Rights of the Child 1989

This international agreement recognises the child and their rights. Children have the right to:

» be heard and listened to

» be consulted on issues that concern them

» be protected from violence

» education

» play

» be free from slavery or financial exploitation

» be protected from abuse

» be cared for and supported if they have disabilities.

Every Child Matters

This government programme lists five key entitlements for children:

» Being healthy – every child has the right to have a healthy lifestyle, including physical and mental health

» Staying safe – every child should be protected from harm

» Enjoying and achieving – every child should be given the opportunity to achieve in life

» Making a positive contribution – every child should have the chance to make a positive contribution to society and avoid getting involved in criminal activity or anti-social behaviour

» Economic well-being – every child has the right not to be held back by being poor.

Criminal Justice Act 2003

This law relates to the power of the police. It looks at criminal offences, bail, sentencing and issues to do with releasing people on licence.

Codes of practice

Codes of practice are rules and guidelines, set by various bodies, on how we should provide services and how we should treat people in our care. Codes of practice relate to the standards we must observe when working with adults, children and young people.

Those who set these standards and develop codes of practice include:

» professional councils – (in which practitioners form a professional group and agree the standards that should be followed)

» regulation and inspection bodies such as Ofsted (Office for Standards in Education) and CHAI (Commission for Healthcare Audit and Inspection)

» legislation which outlines minimum requirements.

GSCC code of practice for social care workers

All those who work in social care must join a register. This register is being introduced slowly. It has started to register all social workers and eventually it will include all those who work in care – such as residential child care workers. When professionals join and put their name on the register they agree to follow a code of practice (a set of rules on how they will behave and operate in the setting).

They will agree to:

» treat all service users as individuals

» apply the rules of confidentiality

» be honest and trustworthy

» keep up to date and attend training

» work as part of a team

» share relevant information with other professionals.

Commission for Social Care Inspection (CSCI)

This organisation registers and inspects voluntary and private care services to ensure that the standards set by either laws or codes of practice are being followed.

The Healthcare Commission – Commission for Healthcare Audit and Inspection (CHAI)

This organisation inspects and assesses standards of health care. It also carries out investigations into serious incidents (for example, deaths in hospitals).

Ofsted (Office for Standards in Education)

Ofsted is responsible for inspecting and assessing standards in education.

ASK

Using the Internet, or other sources, look at the Criminal Justice Act 2003. Make a list of what are seen as criminal offences and what the rules are concerning releasing people on licence.

LINKS

Using a computer, produce a pie chart which shows the percentage of crimes that are normally committed by young people.

Discuss with other learners whether ASBOs (Anti Social Behaviour Orders) work in stopping young offenders committing crimes.

@work

» Ask staff what laws they have to follow to ensure that people's rights are given priority.

» Ask to see a copy of the setting's equal opportunities policy.

» Ask how they put this equal opportunities policy into practice (i.e. what they do on a day to day basis).

Knowing how different values might be supported in a variety of settings within the sectors

Putting policies into practice – what people have to do on a day to day basis ↙

When you work in sectors such as social care, health, child care or justice, you will find that the majority of settings will have:

» an equal opportunities policy

» a policy on protection of children and vulnerable adults

» a confidentiality policy

» an admission policy

» an induction policy

» an advocacy policy

» an anti-harassment and anti-bullying policy

» a complaints policy.

Policies will state the overall aim and intentions of the organisation. However, how policies are put into practice may vary from sector to sector and from setting to setting.

Working with children and young people

On a day to day basis those who work with children and young people will try to protect the rights of individuals by:

» treating all children and their families as individuals

» valuing differences

» challenging discrimination

» promoting positive images of all children and their families

» consulting with children on issues that affect them

» listening to children

» providing diets that are multi-cultural

» providing toys and dressing-up clothes which represent all communities – for example saris to dress up in

- » providing activities that are age- and stage-appropriate (i.e. suited to the age and abilities of the child)
- » employing staff from a variety of backgrounds
- » working in partnership with parents – including all parents regardless of background
- » welcoming people and valuing what they bring
- » trying to learn from other people
- » avoiding stereotyping people – i.e. not making assumptions about them
- » examining the attitudes of staff
- » supporting staff, children and their families who may have been discriminated against
- » developing children's confidence and self-esteem
- » stopping any form of bullying
- » asking what the child likes, and not assuming, for example, that all Asian children are Muslims
- » teaching children to stand up for themselves
- » empowering children
- » celebrating different festivals
- » keeping information confidential on a need to know basis (i.e. they will tell people if the child is in danger)
- » making necessary adaptations for those with special needs
- » not judging people
- » using an interpreter and translating printed information into different languages
- » appointing a key worker.

Working in the care and health sectors

A lot of the principles in child care also apply to adults and you will find the practice very similar. However additional factors will need to be taken into account.

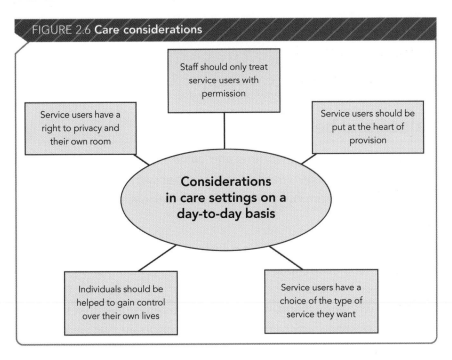

FIGURE 2.6 **Care considerations**

Staff should only treat service users with permission

Service users have a right to privacy and their own room

Service users should be put at the heart of provision

Considerations in care settings on a day-to-day basis

Individuals should be helped to gain control over their own lives

Service users have a choice of the type of service they want

TEAMWORK

Recently the police have had their powers extended. They now have the right to stop and search people who are acting suspiciously. Have a class discussion on whether the police should have this power.

Try to describe a person who looks suspicious. Will the police stop certain groups of people? Try to give reasons for your viewpoints.

@work

» Look for visual signs of how the organisation is putting diversity into practice.

» Try to listen to how staff empower service users.

» Look to see if staff challenge discriminatory practice.

Being able to reflect on your own principles and values in relation to the work of the sectors

Values and beliefs

We all have different viewpoints and value different things. One person will want to get married and another will not. We normally learn our values from our parents and the people around us when we are young.

People who belong to different cultures and groups value different things. In many Asian households (though not in all) marriages will be arranged. In the UK we believe that young people have the right to choose who they marry. It is important to remember that there is no right and wrong way to do things. It is important that we respect differences and understand that people do things differently.

Reflective practice

When you reflect on practice you are generally doing the following:

» looking back at an event or activity that you were involved in

» identifying what went well

» identifying what went badly

» identifying how you can improve in the future.

THINK

"In the UK, Afro-Caribbean men consistently have the highest conviction rates for crime...followed by the white community...then Asians."

What do you think about this statement?

Do you think that Afro-Caribbean men are more likely to be criminals than men in other racial groups?

Are they more likely to be stopped by the police than men in other racial groups?

Do we have negative views about men in this racial group? Are these racist views?

THINK

"Women form half (50%) of the world's population. However, they receive just 10% of the world's income and own less than 1% of the world's property."

Is this fair? Do men have more power than women? Should women stay at home and look after their children?

When we reflect on our own values and the principles of the sector we are trying to see if they are the same. We are reflecting honestly on our attitudes. Everyone has values and we should not be embarrassed. What is important is that we face up to our assumptions and try to change our behaviour.

REFLECT

"Once a junkie, always a junkie." " Can a leopard ever change its spots?"

Discuss what is meant by these statements. What do you think? Can people ever change?

Practice in the Justice Sector is based on the notion that people can be rehabilitated (that is, they can be helped to change their behaviour). What was your attitude when discussing these statements?

MANAGE

Reflect on your own attitudes.

Make a list of all the beliefs and values you have. Be honest with yourself. Examine whether you have any attitudes that are not in line with the principles of the sector. For example, do you think it is wrong to have a child outside of marriage? Do you think it is wrong to be attracted to someone of the same sex?

Make a list of the actions you will need to take to resolve this conflict.

Do you need to become more informed?

What strategies could you use to help you change some of your viewpoints?

... a diversity officer

Name: Samina Khan

Age: 40 years

Salary: £40,000 per annum (per year)

Employer: Local authority social services department

Hours of work: 35 hours per week (7 hours per day)

» Roles and responsibilities (what I do in my job as a diversity officer):

– I am responsible for training people in the organisation on diversity (making sure everyone is treated fairly and showing people how to do this on a day to day basis)
– I am responsible for designing and writing the policies and procedures that the department will follow
– I support staff who feel they have been discriminated against (picked on or bullied because of their gender, race, religion, or sexuality)
– I investigate allegations made by service users. I have to identify whether staff have been discriminatory and have acted inappropriately
– I make sure all staff feel valued
– I have to report any concerns to my manager

» Qualifications:

A degree in social studies
CQSW (social work qualification)
MA cultural studies

» What I like about my job:

Every day is different. I like training and changing the attitudes of people. On the whole people are open to new ideas and are eager to learn about best practice.

» The hardest part of my job:

Some of the most difficult bits about my job are seeing the damage that has been done through discrimination. People who are discriminated against can often lose confidence and it destroys how good they feel about themselves. I have seen very young children and the elderly really confused and distressed because everything around them is unfamiliar to them. Simple things like multi-cultural diets would make people feel more comfortable.

Samina Khan

In the Community

Residential Care →

Rashid is 79 years old and in residential care for the first time. His daughter has been his main carer but she is finding it difficult to manage since having a baby. Rashid is nervous about his new home. He is Asian and likes traditional Asian food and culture. Rashid does not speak English.

» What can the staff do to make Rashid feel comfortable?

» How can the staff treat Rashid with dignity and respect?

» What food could be prepared for Rashid?

» Why is it important to consider these issues?

Questions

Prepare a leaflet for other learners identifying the dietary requirements of someone who is:

– Muslim

– Sikh

– Hindu

– Jewish

Assessment Tips

To pass your assessment for this unit you will need to consider carefully all the information in this chapter and all the information that has been given to you by your teacher.

FIND OUT

» Find out what is meant by key terms such as rights, responsibilities, diversity and equality. You will need to make sure that you identify why these are important when working with people. Draw up a chart which identifies the meaning and the importance of the term.

» You will need to understand what is meant by confidentiality. Why is it important and what are the consequences of breaking this rule? Reflect on how you would feel if people discussed your problems with everyone else.

» You will need to understand about the laws that protect people, such as the Sex Discrimination Act, the Human Rights Act, the Children Act, the Age Discrimination Act, the Care Standards Act and the Criminal Justice Act. You will also need to know about the different codes of practice and give examples of how they support the values of the sector. You will need to identify one piece of legislation and mention one code of practice for each of the four sectors.

» You will need to understand how to put the values of the sector into practice in the setting – for example, treating everyone with respect, providing food from different cultures, keeping and storing information correctly.

» You will need to reflect on your own values and beliefs and how they might relate to the sector. You will need to dig deep and be honest with yourself.

SUMMARY / SKILLS CHECK

» Rights

✓ People in the UK have rights, but they also have responsibilities to and for each other and their communities.

✓ People have a right to: a good education – to be healthy – to vote – to freedom of expression – to a fair trial – to marry – to respect for private and family life – to be free from harm and torture – to be protected from discrimination – to privacy and confidentiality.

» Legislation that protects the rights of the individual

✓ Human Rights Act 1998

✓ Sex Discrimination Act 1975

✓ Race (Amendment) Act 2000

✓ Care Standards Act 2000

✓ Children Act 2004

✓ Disability Discrimination Act 2005

✓ Mental Capacity Act 2005

✓ Age Discrimination Act 2006

✓ Conventions on the Rights of the Child 1989

✓ Every Child Matters

✓ Criminal Justice Act 2003

» People who maybe discriminated against

✓ Certain people in society are more likely to be discriminated against than others, for example: young people – old people – lone parents – the unemployed – ex-offenders – travellers – the homeless – refugees – people who cannot speak English – people from different ethnic groups – women.

» Effects of discrimination

✓ Discrimination can effect people in different ways. They may become: depressed or withdrawn, angry or aggressive. They may feel anxious, disillusioned, worthless and lose their self-esteem, and sense of identity. Some people may switch off and not achieve their full potential in life.

» Values

✓ Values that are important when working with people include: confidentiality, equality of opportunity, treating people with respect and dignity, consultation, continual professional development, working in partnership, reflective practice.

OVERVIEW

This unit has been written to help you learn about partnership working. Working in partnership means planning and providing services from a variety of sectors in a co-ordinated way – for example, a young teenage mother may need support from social services, the school, housing services and the health visitor.

When we work in partnership with others it means that we all talk to each other and plan from a variety of perspectives to ensure that all the needs of the individual service user are met.

Working as a team means that you are working in partnership with others to try to achieve the same thing. Partnerships also involve different teams working together. It isn't always easy to make sure that everyone works together well, especially when each team will have their own priorities, targets and expectations of results from their actions.

Within the community, the same event may require input from several different teams. For example, a road accident may require the ambulance service and police service to work together.

When working in a team, you should always think about the way you work and any improvements that you could make both when working with your own team and with other teams.

03

Working Together

Job watch

You will need this knowledge if you are considering a career as a:

» social worker
» GP
» district nurse
» occupational therapist
» physiotherapist
» warden in sheltered housing
» care worker
» care manager
» early years practitioner
» play worker
» health visitor
» police officer
» community safety officer
» Connexions adviser
» foster carer
» learning mentor
» court advisory worker
» Sure Start worker.

Skills list

On completion of this unit, you should:

» Know different partnerships that provide services in your own community

» Know what is meant by partnership working

» Understand the ways in which individuals receiving services are involved in decision making

» Understand the purpose of teams and the role of the individual within a team, and across teams

» Be able to work collaboratively to solve problems.

Knowing about the different partnerships that provide services in your own community

FIGURE 3.1 **Care professionals meet frequently to share information**

Partnership working involves people from a variety of sectors getting together to share information, knowledge, experience and advice to meet the needs of individuals and their families. Partnership working does not have to take place face to face – it can be done through e-mail, teleconferences and reports. Partnerships, networks and collaborative working play an important role in improving the quality of services provided for individuals and their families. By working with others from a variety of sectors we can co-ordinate the services that are provided for a particular individual.

Examples of partnerships in your local area

In your local area there will be an assortment of organisations who work together in a variety of ways. Some will have regular meetings. Others, such as **children's centres**, will work together in the same building.

Children's centres

When children die at the hands of others there is normally an inquiry. In 2000 a child called Victoria Climbié was horrifically killed by her aunt. When Victoria died, an inquiry was held. The inquiry found that Victoria had been seen by a number of professionals in the different sectors but they had failed to pass information on to the others. Victoria was not given the help she needed because no one had a full picture from all the different organisations about the extent of the abuse she suffered.

Following the Victoria Climbié inquiry the government introduced a new law: the Children Act 2004. The Children Act 2004 requires local authorities to make arrangements for key organisations from the different sectors to work together so that children and young people are looked after properly.

In response to this legislation children's centres where set up in local areas. Children's centres normally employ a range of professionals who work in the same centre and provide the following services:

» nursery provision for children aged 0–5 years

» health visitor

» psychologist

» speech therapist

» GP

» adult learning for parents

» parenting programmes.

On your own, try to find out what is meant by the term *multi-disciplinary working.*

Psychiatric units for adolescents

In the health service a psychiatric unit for young people will have a variety of professionals from the different sectors working together – for example:

» doctors   » family therapists

» nurses   » teachers

» psychologists   » social workers.

Extended schools

By 2010 extended schools should be available to all children. Extended schools will be open all year round from 8am until 6pm. Schools will work with other organisations, both private and voluntary, to provide a variety of services, such as:

» homework clubs

» sport and music clubs

» childcare from 8am until 6pm – this includes breakfast clubs and play centre facilities for after-school hours

» parenting classes

» family support services

» adult learning classes.

Connexions Service

Connexions is a service for young people aged 13–19 years. It provides advice for young people to help them get to where they want to be in life. It also provides services and support for people aged up to 25 years if they have disabilities.

Connexions is a modern public service and young people are actively involved in its design and delivery. The service is managed locally by Connexions Partnerships which bring together all the key youth support services.

Connexions Direct

Connexions Direct is part of the Connexions Service. It provides telephone advice and support for young people aged 13–19 years. It is similar to ChildLine (a 24-hour helpline for children and young people) and it is confidential. Connexions Direct offers young people information on a wide range of topics, as well as confidential advice and practical help. All calls to Connexions Direct are free from a landline and an adviser will ring you back on your mobile.

Advisers will never press you to give your name or personal details. They will not share any information about you outside Connexions Direct unless the adviser thinks you or another young person are in danger or at risk. However, if you wish, they will share your information with specialist organisations who can help you further.

National Strategic Partnership Forum

Community and voluntary groups play an important role in health and social care delivery. They support service users and carers in a variety of ways. Local community groups are a vital source of expertise. Primary Care Trusts are responsible for providing health and social care services and they should work in partnership with local community groups.

The National Strategic Partnership Forum was set up to co-ordinate the partnership arrangements of the different sectors and to help them work effectively together. The National Strategic Partnership Forum reports directly to ministers. It has members from the VCS (voluntary care sector), NHS, Social Care and the Department for Health.

Partnerships with parents

When we work with children it is also important that we work in partnership with parents. Parents know their children better than anyone else. Parents have rights and responsibilities and it is important that we respect them as key players in the life of the child.

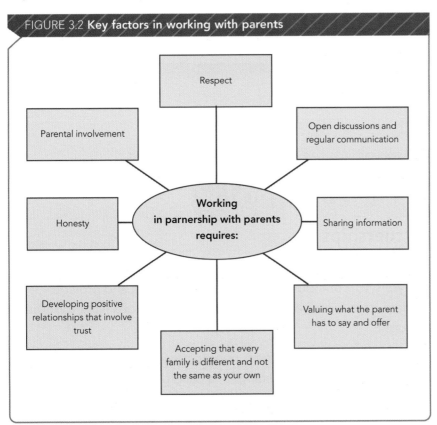

FIGURE 3.2 **Key factors in working with parents**

With someone in your class, research into one partnership arrangement in your local area. Try to find out how one particular organisation works in partnership with others. Use the Internet, books and leaflets, or you could try writing a letter to your local children's department for information.

Prepare a presentation for the rest of the group.

» Ask people in the setting how they work in partnership with other organisations.

» Look to see if professionals from other organisations work in the setting.

Knowing what is meant by partnership working

Partnerships

There are different types of partnerships. It is not possible for everyone to work together in the same building and provide services from a central point. Various organisations work together through:

» Multi-agency panels – here, people meet regularly to discuss issues of concern. For example, a child protection panel will include different professionals – such as a GP, police officer, social worker, teacher – as well as the child's parents

» Multi-agency teams – here, different people provide different services. For example, a young person in a psychiatric unit will need health care (nurses, doctors) and they will need a social worker – they may also need to be referred to a substance misuse worker, and they may need housing

» Integrated services – extended schools and children's centres are examples of integrated practice

» Networks – these are informal and formal groups of people who have knowledge, expertise and understanding of service users in a variety of contexts.

Benefits of working in partnership with others

Partnership working enables organisations:

» to improve service delivery

» to share good practice – to identify and share what works and what does not work

» to improve the quality of services on offer

» to share risks and responsibilities

» to ensure that the individual's needs are being met

» to ensure that services are streamlined and not duplicated

» to ensure that time and money are not wasted

» to ensure that everyone is involved and their views are heard

» to get a total picture (holistic view) of the service user and their needs.

Partnerships that do not succeed

Working together can be difficult. It takes a really committed and skilled worker to work successfully with others. Partnerships can fail if:

» people do not have the correct communication skills and tools – for example, you need to have computers that are compatible (if messages and documents cannot be sent then communication will break down)

- » individuals are not committed and fail to turn up at meetings

- » people do not use the same documentation and information can be misinterpreted. For example, in children's services, the Common Assessment Framework has been introduced – this means that every professional in every sector records information on a child at risk on the same type of form

- » professionals feel intimidated

- » professionals think their service is more important than others (hierarchies)

- » people compete with each other

- » professionals do not contribute and do not follow up actions

- » professionals do not have common goals and aims.

TEAMWORK

In groups of three, use the Internet to research a national partnership arrangement. Identify what organisations are involved and their key aims and objectives

Record your findings on an audiotape which could be given to another learner who has difficulty reading

Ask the staff in your work placement how they work in partnership with other professionals and organisations.

Understanding the ways in which individuals receiving services are involved in making decisions

Decision making

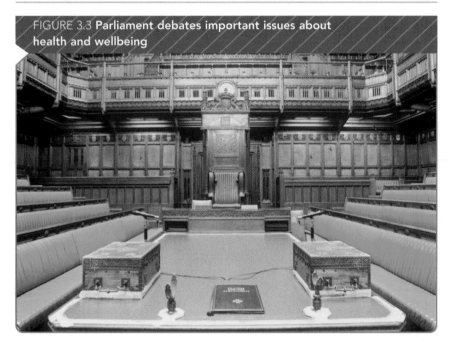

FIGURE 3.3 **Parliament debates important issues about health and wellbeing**

Everyone in the UK over the age of 18 years has the right to vote. The government is elected by the majority. The party which gets the most votes will make decisions for the rest of the country on key issues such as health, education and the provision of goods and services. We as members of the public vote for the party we think will make the right decisions for the country as a whole.

Different parties campaign prior to any general election – they state what they believe in and what they plan to do if they are elected. We also hold local elections and vote for people who will represent our views. By voting we are expressing what we value and our viewpoints on key issues. By voting we are involved in the decision making process.

There are lots of different ways in which we can get the viewpoints of others and involve them in decision making. We can find out other people's viewpoints through:

» voting

» interviews

» surveys

» observations

» consultations

» national and local forums

» national and local networks

» direct questioning

» complaints procedures

» questionnaires.

THINK

The present government is thinking about increasing the school leaving age to 18 years. Do you think this is a good idea or not?

In pairs write a letter to the Minister for Education outlining what you think about this decision. Give reasons for your viewpoints.

Different ways of involving service users in decisions that concern them

When we work with service users – such as families, carers, children, young people, older people, multi-racial groups, people with disabilities, victims and offenders – it is important to involve them in the decisions that are taken about them and their care. Some ways of involving service users are:

» by talking to them and asking their opinions

» by involving them in the care planning process

» through feedback and complaints procedures

» through observations, direct questioning and interviews

» through regular communication, with formal and informal meetings

» by valuing everyone's contribution

» by being clear about the roles and responsibilities of all individuals involved

» by empowering people

» by allowing them to purchase their own care (direct payments)

» by not assuming that we are better than anyone else.

After talking to everyone involved, a plan can be made to include all the services that may be needed – and how they are to be delivered. In a health and care setting, a care plan is a legal document.

» Look to see how staff consult with service users.

» How does the setting record the needs and preferences of those with limited communication skills?

» Do the staff have meetings with service users both formally and informally?

Cathy

Cathy is 36 years old. She lives in a three-bedroom flat in an inner city area. Cathy has three children and is a single parent. She does not work. Cathy suffers from depression following the birth of her last child. She spends the majority of her time in the flat in her dressing gown. She feels that she has no energy or enthusiasm.

Cathy's children are aged 9 months, 4 years and 10 years. Her 4 year old is doing well at school. However her 10 year old has lots of problems. He is bullied by the other children in the class and he has been refusing to go to school. He suffers from dyslexia and finds it difficult to read and write.

FIGURE 3.4 **Cathy has many concerns**

Cathy's elderly mother also lives with her following the death of her father. Cathy's mother suffers from arthritis and has difficulty moving about. Cathy is reluctant to get help because she is worried that social services may take over and take her children away.

With another learner, read the above case study and try to answer the following questions:

» What services and help may Cathy need?

» What help does her 10 year old son need?

» What services and help does Cathy's mother need?

» Will social services take over and take Cathy's children away?

» How can the different organisations involve Cathy, her 10 year old son and her mother in decisions that may concern them?

Understanding the purpose of teams and the role of individuals within teams and across teams

Purpose of teams

When you work in any type of setting in the social care, health, justice, or children and young people's sectors you will be involved in working as part of a team. Working with others is a skill you must learn. You may not like all the people you work with but it is important that you act professionally at all times.

When you work as part of a team you will all have different roles to fulfil in order to meet the needs of all the service users in your care. The purpose of working in a team is:

» to meet the different needs that service users may have

» to share good practice within teams and across teams

» to meet the aims and objectives of the organisation

» to establish common goals and boundaries

» to share expertise

» to share responsibility and risks

» to support each other.

Skills needed for successful teamwork

Trust is an essential ingredient when forming working relationships and working as part of a team. Workers in the health and social care sector have a responsibility to each other. We must be reliable, dependable and honest with each other.

When you work as part of a team you will need to:

» have shared aims and objectives – you all need to agree on the best approach and your plans for the future

» be consistent in your approach across the team – service users will get confused if you all do things differently

» be honest and open

» be sensitive to other members of the team

» hold regular team meetings

» have a behaviour policy for staff

» be open to criticism from other team members

» communicate effectively

» have shared values

» listen to others

» co-operate with others

» share ideas – do not keep things to yourself

» share responsibility

» trust each other

» all pull your weight

» contribute to team meetings

» tell your line manager if you are unhappy

» record formal minutes when you have team meetings

FIGURE 3.5 **Successful teamwork**

» make sure everyone has a say

» understand how to deal with issues sensitively

» make sure you ask for help from another team member if you are unsure about anything

» never allow personal feelings to take over

» be willing to negotiate

» be fair and considerate

» understand the limits of your own role

» make sure you do not try to do the job of another professional – it can be dangerous.

Communication in teams

FIND OUT

What do you think happens when people do not talk to each other? How might this affect the care a service user receives?

Providing a good service depends on communication with service users and other colleagues. It is important that all workers in the health, social care, justice, and children and young people sectors:

» talk to each other

» keep each other up to date with what is happening in different parts of the service user's life

» back each other up and support each other in the event of an emergency

» find time to discuss important issues

» express any doubts and concerns.

Team meetings

Team meetings should take place regularly within teams and across teams. At team meetings there will usually be:

» an *agenda* – this states what you will be discussing in the meeting. It normally gives the following information:

  – the date and time of the meeting

  – a list of those present

  – apologies

  – minutes from the previous meeting

- agenda items – this could be a long or short list

- any other business

» a *chair* – the chair is the person who keeps the meeting in order. They ensure that everyone has their say and that all the items on the agenda are discussed

» *minutes* from the previous meeting – team members will usually have a copy of the notes that were taken at the last meeting. The minutes should highlight any actions that should have been taken

» a *minute taker* – it is important that a member of the group takes notes on any decisions that are made and actions that need to be taken.

TEAMWORK

Choose one of the following topics:

School dinners

School holidays

School breaks

In groups of four, hold a meeting to discuss your topic. Create an agenda, and decide who should be the chair and minute taker.

Make a list of actions that need to be taken following your discussion. Write a set of minutes that could be given to your teacher.

Team evaluation

Team Evaluation
Lawrence Learning Centre
January 2008

Details of team activity
Outing to shops with group of service users who have learning disabilities

My role
To write a letter from the centre to the service users' families to

gain permission for the service user to go on the outing and also identifying what resources they must bring to the centre on the day of the outing, and to escort and be the key person for two of the service users on the outing

How did I perform?

I was happy with the letter that I wrote, and all the service users turned up in appropriate clothing and with the right resources for a day out

How did the team perform? Did we achieve the task?

The team worked hard and they all pulled their weight. However, although we achieved the task we argued between ourselves about the shops we should go into

My strengths

I think I am good at consulting with others and I am good at negotiating. I was able to help others come to a decision about the shops we should go into

Weaknesses

I think the team did not plan enough. We needed to think beforehand about the shops we were going to visit. The team should have consulted with the service users to find out where they would like to go

TEAMWORK

Look at the team evaluation above. In groups of four, take part in a team activity. It could be a meeting, or a planned activity such as a visit to a setting or an outing to the shops, or it could be a presentation that you have to give to other learners in the group

Make a list of the roles and responsibilities of each team member and evaluate how your activity went. Make sure you identify what went well and what needs to be improved

» Look to see if the setting has team meetings

» How often do staff meet as a team?

» Do they invite service users to the meetings?

» Do they have an agenda?

» Look to see if they have minutes from previous meetings.

Being able to work collaboratively to solve problems

Setting goals

When we work with others it is important that we all work towards the same goals. We should all sit down and agree in advance what these should be. When we set goals as a team it is important that they are **SMART**. Smart stands for:

Specific – the goal should be clear and to the point, and not too difficult

Measurable – you should be able to see if you have achieved your goal

Achievable – your goal must be achievable. It should not be so hard that you cannot possibly achieve it

Realistic – you should set a realistic goal. You should not be over-ambitious, or the chances are you will not achieve it

Time scale – you must be realistic about the time scale. If a task takes three days to complete you should not try to do it in a day.

THINK

Set yourself a goal using the Smart objectives listed above. For example, if you are shy you may decide to talk to people more. You could set yourself the goal of talking to one new person a week. This would be specific, measurable, achievable, realistic, and it would have a time scale – one person a week.

Solving problems

Whatever sector you are working in, you will come across problems in your day-to-day work. The most effective way of solving problems is to:

» identify the problem – what is the real issue?

» identify alternative ways of looking at the problem

» identify possible ways forward – a range of solutions should be explored

» identify – taking everything into account – what is the best way forward.

Individuals and groups have very different values and beliefs; for example, some individuals believe that smacking children is an acceptable form of discipline.

Look at the most effective ways of solving problems listed above. Reflect on the main issues involved in smacking children. Are there other ways of looking at this issue? Are there alternative methods of discipline that can be used? What is the best way of disciplining children?

Feedback

A key skill when working with others is giving and receiving feedback. We need to be open to feedback if we are to improve the way in which we work.

Receiving feedback
When receiving feedback about your performance, it is important to:

» listen carefully to what is being said without interrupting

» check that you understand what is being said to you – summarise and if necessary ask for clarification

» ask questions and ask for examples if you do not understand

» think it over – do not get angry, they may have a point

» accept compliments.

Giving feedback
When giving feedback, it is important to:

» be sensitive to the person's feelings

» check they understand what you are saying

» try to find something positive to say

» identify where they need to improve

» be clear.

FIGURE 3.6 **We should accept and learn from all comments made**

REFLECT

Think back to a time when a teacher has had to give you negative feedback. How did it make you feel? How could it have been handled differently?

TEAMWORK

In pairs, produce a glossary (dictionary) of terms for other learners. Your glossary should include definitions of what is meant by the following terms:

* collaboration
* perspectives
* supervision
* goals

* partnerships
* professionals
* community
* multi-disciplinary

... a fire officer

Name: Nick Colney

Age: 47 years

Salary: £35,000 per annum (per year)

Employer: Local Authority Fire Service

Hours of work: 35 hours per week (7 hours per day)

›› Roles and responsibilities (what I do in my job as a fire officer):

- I am responsible for fire safety and visit different organisations to give talks on how they can make the workplace safe
- I am not involved any more in active fire duty. I am not a firefighter
- The fire service is responsible for reducing youth crime in the local area
- I teach young people from the local school basic fire skills. A group of 14 year olds attend the fire station once a week for three hours. We train them and they gain a level 1 BTEC in Fire Safety
- I give talks to schools about the hazards and dangers of fires and the problems that can occur through hoax calls

›› Qualifications:

A degree in English
NVQ Level 3 Emergency Fire
Services – Control Operations

›› What I like about my job:

I like working with young people. I like to see young people change their behaviour and do well in life. When the young people first attend the sessions at the station they are uninterested and despondent. When they leave they have changed and are eager to learn in life. Some young people like to learn by doing. The fire service is a great way of involving young people in the community. We have seen some young people go on to become firefighters after they have attended our sessions.

›› The hardest part of my job:

The hardest part of my job is seeing the damage that can be caused by fire. I find it hard to cope with people who make hoax calls. This wastes firefighters' time and people who genuinely need help suffer.

Nick Colney

In the Community

Andover School →

Andover school is an extended school. It is open from 8am until 6pm all year round. It has been given money from the government to extend its services to the local community.

Those who attend the school live in the local area. Most of the children live on the local housing estate where there are high levels of unemployment, high levels of crime and high rates of drug and alcohol misuse.

The school provides: a breakfast club, an after-school club, a homework club, parenting classes, computer classes, help with form filling as well as a club to help people get back to work.

Questions

1. How might children in the local area be at risk?

2. What are the benefits of providing an extended school service?

3. What might happen to the children in this school if these services were not provided?

4. Make a list of the different professionals who might be employed in this school

Assessment Tips

To pass your assessment for this unit you will need to consider carefully all the information in this chapter and all the information that has been given to you by your teacher.

Create a Word file for your work and remember to include in your headers and footers your name, candidate number, centre name, centre number, the date and the page number.

FIND OUT

» You will need to find out about two different organisations in your local area that work in partnership. You will need to do some research and find out as much information as you can about these two organisations. Remember to focus on how they work with other professionals to benefit service users. You could present your findings in the form of a leaflet.

» You will need to know what is meant by partnership working. You will need to demonstrate that you fully understand what partnership working means.

» You will need to identify two ways in which individuals who are receiving services are involved in making decisions about themselves.

» You will need to find out the purpose and benefits of team working. You will need to take part in a team event and identify the roles of each team member. Team events could include meetings, care planning sessions, parent evenings.

» Once you have taken part in a team event you will need to document how the event was planned, and how you worked with others in the group. You will need to identify any problems you had and how these were resolved.

SUMMARY / SKILLS CHECK

» Different partnerships

✔ There are different types of partnerships. Various organisations work together through: multi-agency panels; a multi-agency team and networks.

» Benefits of working in partnerships with others

✔ To improve service delivery

✔ To share good practice

✔ To identify and share what works and what does not work

✔ To improve the quality of services on offer

✔ To share risks and responsibilities

✔ To ensure that services are streamlined and are not duplicated

✔ To ensure that we do not waste time and money

✔ To ensure that everyone is involved and their views are heard

✔ We get a total picture (holistic view) of the service user and their needs.

» Involving services users

We can involve service users in decision making by:

✔ Talking to them and asking their opinions

✔ Involving them in the care planning process

✔ Getting their feedback

✔ Allowing them to purchase their own care (direct payments)

✔ Carrying out observations, interviews and direct questioning

✔ Acknowledging that all individuals have rights and responsibilities and being clear about their roles and responsibilities.

» Purpose of team

✔ To establish common goals and boundaries

✔ To share expertise, responsibility and risks

✔ To meet the different needs that service users may have

✔ To share good practice within teams and across teams.

OVERVIEW

This unit has been written to help you learn about communicating with others. We communicate our thoughts and feelings in many different ways. When we work with other individuals it is important that we understand how messages are passed from one person to another.

People communicate as much by the way they use their bodies as they do by speaking. For example, we all know that yawning can be a sign of boredom rather than tiredness. A person who speaks to you with their arms crossed over their chest may be trying to put a barrier between you and them. We also need to be aware of cultural differences in body language. For example, in the UK it may be thought that someone is not telling the truth if they can't look you in the eye when they are speaking. However, it may be considered disrespectful in some other cultures to make eye contact with the person who is speaking to you.

Some people are unable to communicate verbally or will not be able to speak the same language as you. You will need to develop special skills when dealing with them to ensure their needs are met.

Listening is a very important skill in the communication process. Make sure that you check that you have understood what someone has just said to you by repeating it to them. When listening, you should try not to interrupt the other person unless you need to make sure that you have understood.

Good communication skills are also very important when recording information about service users in any of the care sectors. You need to make clear and accurate records and remember that some records, such as care plans, are legal documents.

Remember that anything a service user tells you is confidential, but you may need to share some information with other individuals in your team, or with professionals in other sectors.

Are We Communicating?

04

Skills list

On completion of this unit, you should:

» Understand different methods of communicating with a range of individuals

» Understand why it is important to use different methods of communication

» Be able to communicate verbally and non-verbally (including listening skills) in specific situations, within and across the sectors and settings

» Know the purpose of record keeping and sharing information

» Be able to complete records accurately and legibly.

Job watch

You will need this knowledge if you are considering a career in any type of setting in the social care, health, justice, or children and young people's sectors:

» doctor
» midwife
» nurse
» early years practitioner
» care worker
» probation officer
» police officer
» community health visitor
» teacher
» youth worker
» psychologist
» childminder
» after school worker
» play worker
» play therapist
» speech therapist.

Understanding about different methods of communicating with a range of individuals

Communication

From the moment that we are born we all need to communicate and tell people what we want and need. If you observe a baby you will see that they begin to communicate by crying. Babies are able from an early age to tell their parents that they are hungry, cold or need their nappy changing.

Different types of communication include:

» expressing our needs and wants through our body language

» using words

» written communication

» listening to what individuals and groups of people have to say

» watching to see how individuals are feeling.

Children develop language and communication skills from those around them. They learn by example and by watching others. Language is not just about spoken language – it also includes body language or non-verbal communication:

FIGURE 4.1 **Communicating with others**

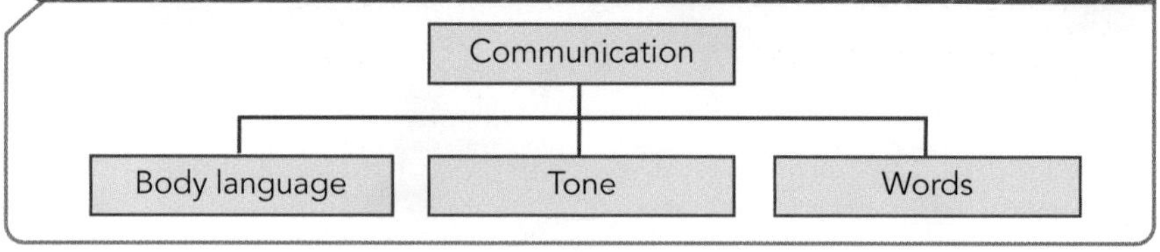

Communication

Body language | Tone | Words

REFLECT

Think back to a time when your parents may have been angry with you. How did you know they were angry if they did not use language? How did they communicate being angry without words? Did they put their hands on their hips? Did they pull a face? Did they stop speaking to you?

The majority of what we say is communicated through our body language and **tone**. We use very little speech to communicate our meaning. We communicate through:

» the pitch of our voice

» volume and tone – how loudly we speak and the harshness of our voice

» eye contact

» facial expressions

» our posture

» touch

» body movements

» muscle tension

» pausing

» crying

» smiling

» taking turns

» how close we are physically to someone

» non-verbal sounds such as grunts and groans.

FIGURE 4.2 **Meaning can be communicated through body language**

TEAMWORK

In groups of three, try to communicate to the rest of the group the following words without using language:

* sad
* happy
* bored
* angry
* love

* hate
* lonely
* distressed
* goodbye
* hello

Once you have done this, identify how babies and people who do not speak English tell you that they are bored, happy, distressed or sad.

Listening skills

A key feature when communicating with other individuals is the ability to listen. When we listen to people, they feel:

» valued

» respected

» important

» treated with dignity

» enabled

» empowered.

When you are listening to other people it is important to be available and to give them your full attention. Do not switch off or allow yourself to be distracted. Show that you are interested in what they are saying through your body language, facial expression, speech and gestures. Be considerate and have a sympathetic approach; showing respect for their views and giving information if requested to do so.

You should observe the other person's expressions and ask questions to check that you have understood what they mean. Use open-ended questions and try not to lead the person or put words into their mouth. Allow people to express themselves in their own manner, words and time.

In conversation, everyone should be allowed to take turns and nobody should take over the conversation.

» Watch how staff communicate with service users.

» How do they communicate with individuals who do not speak – for example, babies?

» Look to see if noticeboards have messages in different languages.

» How do staff communicate with people who cannot hear well?

» Can you identify which communications are formal and which are informal?

Understanding why it is important to use different methods of communication

Language and communication skills are an essential component of who we are. Through communication we learn about ourselves. We develop our sense of self from the reactions of others to us.

If individuals who care for us constantly growl, pull faces and display disapproving feelings we will feel negative and bad about ourselves.

As workers in the care sectors we have a duty to communicate appropriately with a range of individuals who may be in our care.

FIGURE 4.3 **Communication involves more than just talking**

Different methods of communicating

When we work with other individuals in the social care, health, justice and children and young people's sectors we will communicate in the following ways:

- » informal discussions
- » formal meetings
- » in one to one situations
- » in groups
- » team meetings
- » written letters
- » leaflets
- » newsletters
- » reports
- » feedback sessions
- » e-mail
- » telephone
- » memos
- » noticeboards
- » minutes from meetings
- » service user plans
- » observations
- » assessments
- » agreements
- » medical records.

It is important that we check the tone and any hidden messages that we are communicating, even in written format.

Babies and young children

It is important that you are a good role model when communicating with children as they will tend to copy the behaviour of adults who care for them. When talking to babies and young children, you need to be aware that they are more sensitive than adults to body language, gestures and tone of voice. Try to show that you enjoy their company.

You should speak to babies and children calmly, do not shout or raise your voice. Try to make eye contact, position yourself at the child's level if possible, maybe by sitting down. Talk to them when you are giving routine care such as nappy changes or feeding. Give them time and space to respond – even very young babies can smile and coo in response. Show them that you value what they are saying. Make sure you listen to what children say to you. Use open-ended questions and ask their opinion.

You will need to use plain language that children can easily understand. For example, a small child may think if you offer them 'toad-in-the-hole' to eat that they have to eat a toad! You should also be aware of cultural differences. For example, in some cultures it is more polite to burp when you have finished eating than it is to say thank you.

You should take cultural differences into account when offering music, art and craft activities so that children can share their experiences with their carers at home. Children may not speak English at home. So you will need to offer plenty of books and posters in different languages to allow these to be shared at home.

FIGURE 4.4 **Listening at the child's level is important**

Communicating with people who may have English as an additional language

When you are working with service users who do not speak English as a first language it is important to make them feel welcome and comfortable. You may need to offer interpretation services, or translation of written materials. Do speak clearly and at a reasonable pace, allow them to see what is going on around them and check whether they have understood. You may need to show them pictures or point to objects as you say them.

Be careful with your body language. For example, making eye contact with a stranger is considered rude and disrespectful in some cultures. Remember that not being able to speak English, or not speaking it well, does not make someone stupid. Being able to speak more than one language is a skill that should be valued. Do not shout at people who can't speak English – they are not deaf and it will not help them to understand any better.

Think about a time when you may have been abroad on holiday and you could not speak the language. How did you feel asking for something? What would make you feel comfortable in this situation?

Share your views with other learners in the group.

Different methods of communicating and communication aids

FIGURE 4.5 **The first Braille machine was invented in 1892**

British sign language

People who are deaf may not use spoken language. The language used by many deaf people is sign language. British sign language is a system of signs and movements which has been developed by deaf people themselves.

Makaton

Makaton is another form of communication used by people who are deaf. It uses some speech, body language and signs.

Braille

Braille is used by people who are blind. It is a written form of communication. It uses a system of raised dots which enables the blind person to read with their fingers.

Hearing aids

Hearing aids are worn in the ear by people who are hard of hearing. They help people to pick up sounds and signals to aid their hearing.

Speech therapist

A speech therapist works with individuals who have speech problems. They often work with young children and help them acquire speech.

Advocates

Advocates are people who speak on behalf of someone else. If people are not able to speak for themselves – for example they are unconscious, have severe mental health issues or have dementia – then they will have an advocate who looks after their interests. Sometimes the advocate will be a family member.

Translator

A translator is a person who translates written communication into another language. This service is often used by people who do not speak English. Leaflets, letters and important information are translated into the service user's language. Lots of organisations use this service to communicate with people from diverse communities.

Interpreter

An interpreter is someone who will attend a meeting, court, police station, or any other environment where a person cannot speak the language of the country in which they live. An interpreter in the UK will speak English and another language fluently. They will listen in English and translate back to the service user what is being said. The interpreter will then translate what the service user says back into English.

Computers and technology

Technology has improved over the years. Some service users are able to communicate using a computer aid.

ASK

With another learner, research what is meant by sign language, using the Internet.

Design a poster which shows the alphabet using finger spellings. You may find the following websites useful:

www.british-sign.co.uk

www.royaldeaf.org.uk

» Look to see if service users are using communication aids.

» Can staff in the setting use sign language?

» Does the setting employ people who speak more than one language?

Being able to communicate verbally and non-verbally, including listening skills, in specific situations within and across the sectors and settings

Barriers to communication

Sometimes people do not understand what is being said to them. This can be through choice or through no fault of their own. There can be a variety of reasons why people do not communicate.

If you look at the language used by teenagers, they often use slang and jargon by choice. Teenagers enjoy keeping adults out of their conversations. This is part of their growth and development.

There can also be cultural variation in the use of language. People in different parts of the UK often have different terms for the same object. For example, in the north of England people will talk about having a 'butty', while in the south people will call the same thing a sandwich or 'sarnie'.

Some people do not pay attention when they are spoken to, either deliberately or because they are unable to do so. Listening is a skill that needs to be developed when caring for others. Always give the person talking your full attention – try to look at them and make sure that they can see you. Check that you have understood what has been said by repeating key words or phrases.

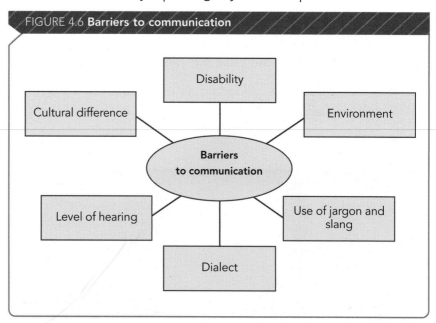

FIGURE 4.6 **Barriers to communication**

Make a list of as many jargon or slang words you use that you can think of. Identify what your slang words mean. Do other learners and your teacher understand what the words mean? When do you use slang and jargon, and who do you use it with?

Do you think we use different types of language when we are with different people?

Does your language change when you talk to your teacher? friends? parents?

REFLECT

Think about strategies you could use to overcome barriers to communication such as:

* jargon and slang

* environmental difficulties, e.g. noise or discomfort

* lack of attention or not listening

* cultural differences

* disabilities, e.g. with sight or hearing.

THINK

Communicating with someone who is aggressive

FIGURE 4.7 **Dealing with aggression**

When we work with other people it is inevitable that at some point we will come across an individual who is angry. People react to situations in different ways. Some individuals who are angry will walk away, others will shout, and others will lash out. It is important that we know how to deal with this situation so that we minimise the risk of harm to ourselves, to others, and to the person who is angry.

It is important that:

» service users are aware of what is acceptable and unacceptable behaviour in the setting

» you understand the triggers that can make a person react aggressively

» you ensure that you are communicating appropriately with all service users

» you do not patronise people or put them down

» you always try to prevent a difficult situation arising if you can – for example, if two children always fight, try to avoid asking them to do something together

» you try to let people sort out their differences, and only intervene if someone's safety is at risk

» you always report incidents to your line manager

» you try to stay calm and in control of your own feelings

» you get help if needed

» you gain the trust of individuals and negotiate – try to understand the viewpoint of the person who is angry

» you gently introduce explanations and ideas for solving the problem

» you do not argue with the individual

» you allow the person time to calm down. You may not be able to discuss issues with them immediately – it may have to wait till later or the next day

» you try to end the discussion on a positive note so that the person feels better about themselves.

In groups of three make a list of ways in which you would communicate with someone who has just recently had a stroke and has limited communication skills. Identify why it is important to communicate with this person.

When you have finished, create a word file for your work. Insert a header and footer showing who the procedure was compiled by and the date. Include the page number.

L I N K S

>> Listen to see if staff are using specialist jargon.

>> Do the service users understand some of the specialist language staff use?

>> Do staff change their tone and use of language with different people in the setting?

>> Observe how they cope with individuals who have disagreements or who may be aggressive.

>> Ask staff what is unacceptable behaviour in the setting.

Knowing about the reasons for keeping records and sharing information

Types of records that might be kept

Records about individuals need to be kept to make sure that everyone involved in their care has access to the same information. For example, the types of records kept may include:

» attendance records

» personal details, such as name, age, address, marital status and information about family members

» contact details, and who to contact in an emergency

» information about allergies and other health-related issues.

Other records that may need to be kept in a care setting are listed below.

Learning agreements (contracts)

This is a contract between a learner and their teacher about behaviour. It will state what is expected from the learner and what the teacher will provide. Agreements are important so that everyone is aware of what is expected.

Medical records

Medical records are generally held by the individual's GP (general practitioner). Each individual will have a file containing information such as:

» name and address

» past health history and previous illnesses and operations

» blood pressure, weight, height, blood type

» family history and illnesses of other family members

» hospitals that the individual has attended

» letters of referral that have been sent to other professionals

» any allergies

» any medication that is being taken

» a record of visits to the doctor and treatment given.

THINK

In groups of three, identify why it is important to keep information confidential. What might happen if information on individuals fell into the wrong hands? Look at a recent case in the media where confidential information has gone missing. How do you think people might feel? Would you want other people to know your personal details?

Observations

All those who work with children and young people must carry out regular observations on those in their care. Observations record the actions of a child within a given time frame.

Observations are carried out for the following purposes:

» to learn about how children develop

» to assess how children are developing as individuals

» as a tool and record to give feedback to parents on the progress of their child

» to identify any difficulties the child may be experiencing

» to plan activities that will help the child in the future

» to inform other professionals about issues of concern

» as a legal document in suspected cases of child abuse

» to identify what children are interested in

» to identify how children are using the environment

» to help understand a child's behaviour.

FIGURE 4.8 **Learning through play**

Care plans

Good practice guidelines and the law state that local authorities have a responsibility to assess those in need. This is normally done through a care plan. Care plans are records which include:

» an assessment of the individual and their needs

» details of the services that will be provided

FIGURE 4.9 **Assessing the service user's needs**

» the risks to the individual if these services are not provided.

When organisations are putting together a care plan for an individual it is important that:

» the care plan is person-centred – that staff draw up the plan in consultation with the service user

» the care plan takes into account the service user's family and culture

» staff consult and respect the views of the service user's family

» the organisation works with other professionals so that a range of services can be provided to meet the needs of service users

» the organisation respects diversity

» there is a system in place to review plans regularly to ensure that service users' needs are being met.

Different people will have different needs and the assessment of service delivery will vary from one individual to another. A key factor with care plans is that this is a contract between the local authority and the service user about the service they are entitled to.

Data Protection Act 1998

When you keep records on individuals it is important that you remember the law and the rights of individuals. The Data Protection Act 1998 states that information must:

» be kept secure

» be accurate

» not be passed to other countries unless it is completely secure

» not be excessive

» be fairly and lawfully processed

» not be kept longer than necessary

» be written for a limited purpose

» be processed in accordance with the individual's rights.

Reasons for sharing information with others

Information may need to be shared with others for the following reasons:

» in order to benefit the service user

» in order to provide a range of services

» if a person is at risk

» it is a legal requirement to work in partnership with other organisations

» so that services can be provided in an integrated way

» in order to inform other individuals on a need to know basis

» so that information about individuals does not go unnoticed.

TEAMWORK

In groups of three, using the Internet research the guidelines that organisations use for sharing information with other organisations. Make a list of who they share information with and what type of information they will pass on. Identify what the government recommends for working in partnership with others.

When you have completed your research use your notes to prepare for a discussion with the rest of the class.

Discuss your findings with the rest of the class.

LINKS

» Ask staff what information the setting holds about individuals, and why.

» Ask how long they keep records about service users.

Being able to complete records accurately and legibly

Why it is important to record information clearly, objectively and accurately

Records need to be clear so that other professionals understand what is being said – information can be misinterpreted by others if it is not clear. It is important to get permission from service users to record information and share it with others.

» It is important to record what we see and not what we think – we must not make assumptions. For example, some individuals may laugh if they are nervous rather than happy.

» The needs of service users will not be met if information is recorded incorrectly.

» Inaccurate inforamtion can be dangerous and put people at risk.

» Signing and dating records shows that the information is a true account and who to contact. Also, a record may be a true account for that date and time but not a true account at a later date.

MANAGE

With another learner, can you think of other reasons why it is important to keep records that are factual, accurate, clear, objective, signed and dated?

I want to be...

... an interpreter or translator

Name: Ahmed Khan

Age: 28 years

Salary: £40,000 per annum (per year)

Employer: Self-employed

Hours of work: Varied – sometimes 20 hours per week, other times 40 hours per week – it depends on the different contracts I receive

» **Roles and responsibilities (what I do in my job as an interpreter and translator):**

– I speak French, German, Spanish and Gujarati
– I am responsible for translating for different organisations that may need my services
– I work in all the sectors and can be called on to translate for those who have been arrested or taken to court, or for those who have witnessed a crime
– I translate at meetings for social services so that service users are clear about what is being said and their viewpoints are expressed and understood by social workers
– I translate for groups of parents at meetings in schools
– I attend meetings to translate when there are areas of difficulty between the service user and the organisation
– I translate written communication – for example, if settings are sending out leaflets or letters they will get me to translate them.

» **Qualifications:**

A degree in French.

» **What I like about my job:**

I like meeting lots of different people. My job is varied and I do not work from nine till five. I like being involved in interpreting for the courts because you get to hear lots and lots of different cases. I feel that I am doing something useful and helping people to communicate. People who do not speak English need support, especially when they have to go to court to give evidence.

» **The hardest part of my job:**

Sometimes I am waiting for work to arrive. I have to take all the work that is offered because I do not know when my services will be needed again, and sometimes that means I end up working long hours. It can take a long time for my payments to be processed by different organisations.

✱ Ahmed Khan

In the Community

Who's talking →

Anthony, a care worker in a residential home for people with severe learning difficulties, is working with Mary, who suffered brain damage at birth. Anthony sits with Mary and sings. Mary nods her head and taps her feet. Anthony walks away and pours a glass of cold water for Mary. He puts the drink to Mary's mouth. Mary pushes the glass out of Anthony's hand and the water goes all over the floor.

Jaspal is a home carer for Tom who is 72 years of age. Tom has severe arthritis and is hard of hearing. Tom has a doctor's appointment and Jaspal goes with him to the surgery. When Tom is called in to see the doctor, Jaspal goes in with him and helps him sit down on the chair. The doctor turns to Jaspal and asks what the problem is. Jaspal tells the doctor that Tom is finding it difficult to get around and he is experiencing severe pain. The doctor writes a prescription for Tom and gives it to Jaspal. They both walk out.

Questions

1. How would you feel if someone just put a drink to your mouth?

2. How would you feel if someone talked over you and did not consult you?

3. What could Anthony and Jaspal do differently next time?

Assessment Tips

To pass your assessment for this unit you will need to consider carefully all the information in this chapter and all the information that has been given to you by your teacher.

Create a Word file for your work and remember to include in your headers and footers your name, candidate number, centre name, centre number, the date and the page number.

FIND OUT

» You will need to understand about different types of communication, and give examples from your own experience of communicating in a one to one situation, in a group situation, and in two different formal and informal situations. For each situation you will need to identify what the communication was about, how successful it was, what verbal skills were used, what messages were given by different people's body language, whether there were any barriers, and how you could improve in the future.

» You will need to demonstrate that you understand the different types of communication that take place with different types of people, and identify why it is important to communicate in different ways. You will need to look at the different types of communication used – for example, communication with babies, using sign language with people who do not have spoken language, written communication, using translators with those who have English as an additional language – and give reasons why it is important to communicate with these groups. You could design a poster which demonstrates through pictures the different types of communication skills used. You could then explain underneath each picture why it is important to communicate in this way.

» You will need to develop your understanding of communication skills in more depth. You will need to plan a discussion that you will have with another person or with a group of people. You will need to identify the purpose of the discussion, the roles of the participants, two potential barriers and how they were minimised, three communication skills used by yourself and others, and how you dealt positively with feedback. Try to plan a discussion with other learners in the group – ask your teacher to observe the discussion and give feedback. Comment on how you felt when the teacher identified your strengths and weaknesses. Draw up a plan of action for improvement.

» For this section of your assignment you will need to know about the records that are kept by different organisations in the social care, health, justice and children and young people's sectors. For each sector you will need to identify one type of record that is kept, the information that will be recorded, why the information is needed, and two boundaries to sharing information in the sector.

» You will need to complete three forms accurately and clearly. You could look at different forms such as your learning agreement with your teacher, feedback sheets, evaluation sheets, records, and notes taken during discussions.

SUMMARY / SKILLS CHECK

» How we communicate

✔ The majority of what we say is through body language and tone. We use very little speech to communicate our meaning.

» Some different methods of communicating

✔ Informal discussions, formal meetings, one-to-one situations, groups, team meetings, written letters, leaflets, newsletters, reports, feedback sessions, e-mail, telephone, memos, notice boards, minutes from meeting, service user plans, observations.

» Why it is important to use different methods of communication

✔ People have the right to be consulted and listened to. Different communication skills are needed with different people to ensure they feel valued and that you understand what they say and need.

» Barriers to communication

✔ Jargon, cultural differences, not speaking English, not being given enough time and space, negative attitudes, disabilities – particularly with speech or hearing, the environment, accents and dialect.

» Different types of records that might be used and kept

✔ Attendance records; personal details – e.g. age, address, family members; likes and dislikes; preferred name; marital status; contact details; who to contact in an emergency; allergies and other related health issues; learning agreements; medical records; observations; care plans.

» Data Protection Act 1998

✔ When keeping records, it is important that you remember the law and the rights of individuals. The Data Protection Act 1998 states that information must be: accurate, only kept if necessary, not excessive and written for a limited purpose, kept securely, not passed to other countries unless it is completely secure, fairly and lawfully processed in accordance with the individual's rights.

» Reasons for sharing information with others

✔ It is a legal requirement to work in partnership with other organisations to provide a range of services in an integrated way to benefit the service user. You may need to share information with another agency if an individual is at risk and needs support that you/your agency cannot provide.

OVERVIEW

This unit has been written to help you learn more about caring for children and adults. When you work with other individuals it is important that you have a basic understanding and knowledge of the factors that may cause them harm or injury. It is essential that children and adults who are cared for by others are kept safe.

You will explore how people become sick or ill and what you can do to stop this happening. For example, you will look at the importance of hand washing and hygiene in the workplace and what are the main causes of infection.

As you have seen in Unit 4, good communication is key to working effectively in the care sectors. In this unit, you will look at the different forms of abuse and the ways in which you can keep vulnerable individuals safe from harm. Your communication skills in recognising other people's body language will help you to identify people who may be being abused. There will be agreed procedures that you are asked to follow both in a work setting and in the community when you suspect that someone is being abused.

Health, safety and security are important in the care sectors both to protect individuals receiving care and also to protect care workers. In this unit, you will explore key legislation protecting both care workers and their carers in the work setting (including working in the community), policies and procedures that ensure safe practice.

By the end of this unit, you should be able to carry out a simple risk assessment in a care setting. For example, you could look at a play activity in a child care setting and assess whether it could be dangerous to the children, or maybe to the staff if equipment needs to be set up before, and put away after, the activity.

Is it Safe?

Skills list

On completion of this unit, you should:

» Understand the main causes of infection

» Understand the ways in which vulnerable people can be protected from harm and abuse

» Know key legislation and regulations that govern health, safety and security

» Know why organisations have policies for health, safety and security, and how these policies protect individuals

» Be able to carry out a basic health and safety risk assessment for a specified setting.

Job watch

It is important that you have some understanding and knowledge of how to keep people safe if you are considering the following careers:

» police officer

» doctor

» dentist

» midwife

» nurse

» health visitor

» early years practitioner

» care worker

» environmental health officer

» probation officer

» youth worker.

Understanding the main causes of infection

There are three main causes of ill health in humans:

(a) Micro-organisms (germs)

(b) Genetics (what you are born with that you get from your parents)

(c) Environment (things around you that can make you ill, such as poor diet, poor housing, drugs, smoking, alcohol).

Germs

A **germ** is a micro-organism that enters the body. A germ can be a bacterium, a virus or a type of fungus. An infection occurs when a germ enters the body and the body reacts. Not all germs are harmful to humans. Illness is the body's reaction and main defence against a germ. Germs can enter the body through:

» the nose

» the mouth

» blood

» touch

» sexual contact

» food and water

» insects and animals.

FIND OUT

Find a simple definition that you can understand for the following:

• bacterium

• virus

• fungus.

Now see if you can find two illnesses caused by each of them. Hint: You could try searching the NHS Direct website – www.nhsdirect.nhs.uk.

Visit your local GP practice or clinic and pick up any leaflets with information about how you can contract HIV. Discuss with your teacher and other learners how you can protect yourself from getting HIV. Discuss why some young people may find it difficult to say 'No' to sexual activity.

Signs of illness in children and adults

When children or adults are ill they will display signs and symptoms that something is wrong. People do not all react in the same way, and it is important that the person caring for an

TABLE 5.1 Illnesses that can be caused by germs

Illnesses and infections	Methods of transmission (how the germ is passed on to others)
Colds, coughs and flu	Sneezing, coughing, speaking, kissing
HIV, hepatitis	Sexual activity, bodily fluids, blood
Food poisoning	Contaminated food, insects, flies
Gastroenteritis (diarrhoea)	Hands, food, sneezing, kissing
Scabies	Touch
Cold sores	Contact, touch
Impetigo	Broken skin, touch
Head lice	Touch, contact
Mumps	Contact, touch, sneezing

DID YOU KNOW?

Colds, flu and hepatitis are usually caused by viruses.

Food poisoning may be caused by bacteria.

Head lice, threadworms and scabies are parasites.

Thrush (Candida) is a fungal infection.

individual recognises the signs of illness. Signs and symptoms can include:

» runny nose
» withdrawn appearance
» aggressiveness
» poor appetite
» change in behaviour
» hot and sweaty appearance
» rash

» crying
» attention seeking
» high temperature
» bed wetting
» sleepiness
» vomiting
» runny eyes
» moodiness
» coughing

» paleness
» red skin tone
» drowsiness
» rapid breathing
» headache
» aches and pains
» bad breath.

Caring for someone who is ill

When children and adults are ill they need comfort and warmth from the person who is caring for them. You should try to:

» comfort the sick person and give them reassurance

» provide regular drinks

» offer them food if they want it

» allow them to stay in bed

» provide simple activities for them to do

» ensure you have followed good hygiene practices

» keep them warm and comfortable

» spend time talking to them

» change their clothes when necessary

» give them a wash or bath

» call the doctor if necessary

» change their bedding when necessary

» ensure an adequate supply of fresh air.

Ways in which you can help prevent the spread of infection and stop people getting ill

To some extent, the spread of infection can be controlled by others, using the following procedures:

Always wash your hands

» after using the toilet

» before preparing or touching food

» after blowing your nose

» after handling animals

» after changing nappies or dealing with waste

» after empting bins

» before carrying out first aid

» after handling other people's bedding, tissues, bodily fluid.

Personal hygiene

» keep yourself clean, and try to bath daily

» brush your hair and teeth daily

» change and wash clothes regularly

» have your own towel, flannel and toothbrush

» use liquid soap

» use paper towels rather then hand towels

» use tissues rather then hankies and dispose of them immediately

FIGURE 5.1 **Hand washing**

» ensure that the room is well ventilated

» do not use empty toilet rolls when doing art activities with children.

Disposing of waste products

» always use disposable gloves when dealing with bodily waste, such as nappy-changing, or treating cuts and wiping up blood

» waste material should be disposed of following the setting's procedures

» nappies should be put in a sealed bag.

THINK

One of the most effective ways we have to protect ourselves and others from illness is good personal hygiene. Design a poster that highlights the importance of personal hygiene and explain why personal hygiene is important in the workplace.

Food hygiene

It is important that all those who work with others follow set procedures to prevent food poisoning:

» All staff who prepare food must have food hygiene training

» Hands must be washed before preparing food

» Hair should be tied back

» Staff should always wear aprons

» Cuts and wounds must be covered with blue plasters

» Worktops must be washed before and after preparing food

» Raw meat should be kept in sealed containers and kept at the bottom of the fridge

» The 'use by' date instructions must be followed

» Frozen foods should be defrosted

» The manufacturer's instructions on labels must be followed

» Frozen foods must not be re-frozen

CHECK IT OUT

Immunisation can protect children and adults from certain diseases. For more information, visit www.nhsdirect.nhs.uk and look up the sections about adult and child immunisation.

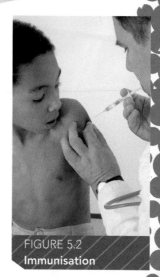

FIGURE 5.2
Immunisation

CHECK IT OUT

Useful websites. Health Protection Agency:

www.hpa.org.uk

www.bupa.co.uk

www.workplacelaw.net

» Left-over food should be given time to cool down and then put in the refrigerator

» Food should be kept covered.

Keeping the workplace hygienic

It is important that the workplace is kept clean and hygienic. People who work with others must always:

» clean work surfaces, tables, chairs, toys and equipment used by others

» sweep and mop the kitchen daily

» clean tables before and after meals

» clean and disinfect toilets daily.

Do not use the same cloth for the toilet and the kitchen. They must be different cloths. Do not use the same brush and mop in the kitchen and the toilet area.

» sweep and mop all areas in the workplace daily

» clean up and mop any spillages immediately

» clean work surfaces before preparing food

» empty bins daily

» clean the nappy-changing area after each nappy-change.

» Ask people in the work setting how they care for someone who is unwell.

» Ask people at work what they would do in an emergency.

» Ask people at work if they have done first aid training.

» Ask people at work if they have attended food hygiene training.

Genetic causes of illness

When we are born we inherit different features from our parents. We acquire these features through our **genes**. Some of the features we can inherit from our parents are shown in Figure 5.3.

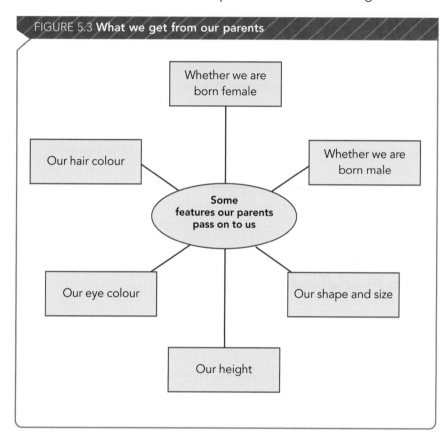

FIGURE 5.3 **What we get from our parents**

- Whether we are born female
- Our hair colour
- Whether we are born male
- Some features our parents pass on to us
- Our eye colour
- Our shape and size
- Our height

CHECK IT OUT

What features you have inherited from your parents. Who do you look like? Do you look like your mum, dad, aunt, uncle or even a grandparent?

We can also inherit illnesses from our parents and grandparents which have been passed down through our genes. Illnesses that can be genetically inherited include:

» cystic fibrosis

» sickle cell anaemia

» Down's syndrome.

Environmental factors which may cause illness

The environment and the way in which we live can have a big impact on our health. Smoking, drugs, alcohol, poor housing, and dirty and unhygienic restaurants can all make individuals extremely sick and in some cases can ultimately result in their death.

TABLE 5.2 Effects of smoking, drugs and alcohol on health

Smoking	Drugs	Alcohol
Death	Death	Death
Asthma, shortness of breath or breathing difficulties	Heart attack	Raised blood pressure
Cancer, heart disease and strokes	Depression, psychosis and hallucinations	Depression
Developmental delay	Hyperactivity, aggression and a lack of self-control	Brain and liver damage
Increase blood pressure	Developmental delay	Malnutrition
Foetal damage (babies can be born small if their mother smokes during pregnancy)	Miscarriage or foetal damage	Lack of self-control and aggression
	Sleeping problems, decreased energy levels and poor concentration	Slow reaction times
	Headaches	Heart disease and strokes
		Foetal damage

» Ask people at work why they cannot smoke on the premises.

» What is the law that relates to smoking at work?

ASK

Some people drink to cope with stress, others drink socially. Talk to adults that you know, and ask them to keep a diary for a week listing what alcohol they drank, when they drank it, why they drank and how much.

* Using the internet, find out how many units of alcohol are safe for adults to consume in a week

* Identify how many units of alcohol each person you spoke to had during the week. Record the information from this activity in a table

* Identify who drinks the most, why they drink, and the likely effects on their health

* Prepare a leaflet that highlights the dangers of alcohol.

Understanding how vulnerable people can be protected from harm and abuse

Most people believe that all individuals have the right to live in a caring and loving environment and that they should not be exposed to harm or abuse. However, there are some people who intentionally abuse others or put them at risk of harm through neglect. Individuals, members of the community, and workers in health care settings and the justice sector have a responsibility or 'duty of care' to protect and report all suspected cases of abuse.

Different types of abuse

People can be abused in many ways and it is important that you recognise signs and symptoms of different types of abuse. It isn't always easy to know whether someone is being abused or whether they have, for example, just hurt themselves or they are always shy and timid. Also, the individual may not complain about what is happening to them. Physical abuse can leave signs such as bruises, cuts, scrapes, burns and even broken bones. However, these may be hidden under clothing. Sexual abuse may show in a child or a very old person having a sexually transmitted disease. (Do not forget that older people may still be sexually active.) You may notice torn or stained underwear. The individual may be withdrawn or aggressive. Other forms of abuse include emotional, an individual who doesn't receive love and affection, or neglect, which can include depriving the individual of basic living needs such as food, shelter, warmth and access to hygiene facilities.

FIGURE 5.4 **Bullying is never acceptable**

Under the headings physical abuse, sexual abuse, emotional abuse and neglect, list as many signs and symptoms that you think an individual might show if they are being abused.

What to do if you suspect abuse or someone tells you they are being abused

» **Listen calmly**. It is important that you stay calm even if you are deeply disturbed by what you hear. The person who is telling you will need your support. They have trusted you completely.

» **Believe what you are told**. If you have never been involved in abuse before it can be hard to believe. However the person telling you (**disclosing**) needs you to believe them.

How would you feel if nobody believed what you were saying?

Do children tell lies?

» **Tell the person in charge**. Every workplace setting will have a person in charge (nominated person) who deals with suspected cases of abuse. It is important that you tell this person so that they can inform the correct department, such as police or social services. It is important that you only tell the person in charge and do not gossip with others about what has happened. Reflect on how you would feel if people had confidential information about you.

Everyone should work as part of a team. By telling the person in charge you are taking full responsibility for your role in that team.

» **Reassure the person**. Tell them that you are glad they have told you and that it is not their fault.

» **Do not judge**. It is not the person's fault and they have a right to live without harm or injury. People who are abused are often frightened and powerless to get away.

» **Tell the person you cannot keep this a secret and you have to inform your supervisor**. You must not make promises you cannot keep. You have a duty to tell the person in charge.

THINK

It is important that you keep whatever you have heard in the setting confidential. You must not tell family members or friends at home. Think of how people would feel if others found out.

» **Do not tell the person everything will be OK – it may not be**. It is important that you listen only. In some cases children may be removed from the home and this may be difficult for them.

» **Write down factually what you are told**. It is important that you record what you hear, not what you think. Your records could be used in a court case.

» **Listen, do not question**. It is important that you do not put words into the other person's mouth. Most of us are not trained as police workers, psychologists or social workers and we could inflict more harm on the person who is disclosing.

CHECK IT OUT

Useful websites

www.kidscape.org.uk

www.nspcc.org.uk

REFLECT

Bullying can be seen as a form of abuse. Reflect back to a time when someone may have picked on you or bullied you.

How did you feel? How did you deal with it? Did you tell anyone? Did you get angry? Did you run away? Did you confront them? Were you frightened?

Record your thoughts on a piece of paper and discuss them with the rest of the learner group.

Produce a list of all the actions you could take if someone was bullying you.

After completing the first part of the task, summarise your findings and, working with another learner, write a letter to your teacher identifying how to support people who may be experiencing bullying in the school.

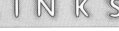

LINKS

» Ask who is in charge when it comes to the protection of vulnerable adults and/or children.

» Ask if they have instructions for staff on how to deal with suspected cases of abuse.

The law and the protection of vulnerable adults and children

There are laws and guidelines to help protect people from harm and abuse. For example, all those who work with vulnerable adults and children must undergo a police check. A police check makes sure that those who come into contact with vulnerable adults and children are safe to work with them – for example it will check that the person has no convictions for crimes such as child abuse and violence.

Key laws and guidelines

» **POVA** (Protection of Vulnerable Adults) – a scheme set up by the Department of Health to stop people who have harmed others in their care from working in the sector. It is a list that professional organisations can check to see if people have committed offences.

» **Criminal Records Bureau** – an organisation responsible for carrying out police checks on professionals.

» **Children Act 1989** – legislation which requires local authorities to provide protection for children in their area.

» **Children Act 2004** – further legislation which requires different agencies to work together to protect children. For example doctors should talk to teachers, the police and health visitors.

» **Every Child Matters** – a government programme which lists five key entitlements for children.

CHECK IT OUT

Visit www.everychild matters.gov.uk to find more information about Every Child Matters. See if you can find out the Government's five key aims for each child.

THINK

Identify why it is important for different departments to talk to each other.

How can departments communicate with each other?

How you can support vulnerable adults and children who may have experienced abuse in the work setting

» Make sure you recognise when someone is being abused

» Make sure you know the rules to follow if you suspect someone is being abused

» Be kind and do not judge

» Allow people to express their feelings

» Allow children to say no if they are unhappy

» Support children to look after their own care/toileting needs

» Talk to people in a way that makes them feel good about themselves

» Teach children about stranger danger

» Make sure unwanted visitors cannot get into the building unnoticed

» Make sure everyone signs in when they visit

» Make sure gates and doors are locked

» Do not insist that children kiss adults goodbye

» Protect yourself – make sure you are never left on your own with a child or vulnerable adult

» Do not gossip – make sure you follow the principles of confidentiality

» Report staff to your supervisor if you think they are abusing clients in their care.

Knowing the key legislation and regulations that govern health, safety and security

Laws have been passed to safeguard people from harm. Over many years the government has identified key areas where people experience harm or increased risk of injury. It is important that all those who work with children and adults have an understanding of the law that protects both staff and members of the public from harm. Those who work with other individuals share the responsibility with their employer for the safety of all people who use the service. (The law has changed and we can no longer place the blame on our employer if an accident happens. We are all responsible.)

What to do if someone has had an accident and is in danger

First aid

It is important that those who work with others have been trained in first aid. If you have been trained and someone is in need of assistance you should:

» stay calm

» assess the situation and make sure that it is safe for you to help

» if it is safe to do so, remove any additional dangers that may pose a threat

» shout for help, or ask someone to go for help and to call emergency services (dial 999)

» deal with the most serious injury first

» check for a response by asking the casualty a question like 'can you hear me?' and gently shaking their shoulders

» if no response, check for breathing

» if casualty is not breathing normally, or you are in any doubt, administer CPR (cardio-pulmonary resuscitation)

» if casualty is unconscious and breathing normally, put them in the recovery position.

TEAMWORK

It is important to have a qualified first aid person in all settings. Anyone who works with people should do some form of first aid training.

In pairs, produce an information leaflet that describes what to do in the following situations:

✱ an unconscious person

✱ a child with a grazed knee

✱ a person who has stopped breathing

✱ a child who is choking

✱ someone who is bleeding heavily

✱ a person who has a suspected broken leg

Using this information, prepare a presentation for the rest of the class that demonstrates how to carry out one first aid procedure.

LINKS

What you can do to ensure the safety of service users in the setting

When working in a care setting – for example, in a nursery – you should check that:

» equipment is safe for use

» toys have the European Community CE mark

» outside areas are safe and free from danger

» floors are dry and free from spillages

» fire exits are clear

» the first aid box is fully equipped

» bins have been emptied

» carpets and rugs are not worn or curled at the edges

» electrical flexes are not trailing across the floor and will not cause people to trip

» cleaning materials are properly labelled and stored safely

» medicines are stored safely

» children's play areas are free from dog and cat faeces

» children's play areas are free from broken glass and needles

» there are no sharp edges that children can fall on

» personal belongings are kept locked away and safe from others.

Watch also for children or staff who may be showing signs of illness.

It is important that staff in all settings report **hazards** (possible dangers) to the person in charge. You should report hazards such as:

» broken equipment

» people acting suspiciously

» fire risks

» broken gates

» reported lost property

» people who are feeling ill.

FIGURE 5.5
Playing safely

Security in the setting

Not all care environments are under lock and key. Adults who are being cared for have the right to walk in and out as they please. This makes security sometimes difficult to manage. However it is important that everyone is vigilant. People need to be aware at all times of what is going on in the setting.

Organisations who look after individuals must consider:

» **Security against intruders**. Security can be improved by means of: badges, microchips, CCTV, keys, named key holders, password schemes, registers for signing in and out, escorting visitors whilst on the premises, and restricted access (only allowing visitors in certain areas). When working with children it is important that gates and entry doors are locked at all times so that no one can enter and children cannot escape.

» **How to challenge intruders**. Always ask who they are. Do not make assumptions that they have a right to be there. Be polite – escort them to their destination. If in doubt raise the alarm.

» **Safe collection of children**. You must never let children go home with someone you do not know (unless you have written permission from the child's parent/carer). If someone you do not know tries to collect a child, take the child with you and report what has happened to the centre manager.

» **Security of property**. All settings should have a property book and policies for the safe storage and collection of valuables and service users' belongings.

TRY THIS

Make a list of the possible dangers to yourself if you challenge an intruder aggressively.

TRY THIS

Think about what you would do if you became aware that a member of staff was stealing from a service user.

» Check that all fire exits in the setting are clear.

» Make a list of the contents of the first aid box.

» Make a list of all the safety symbols in the environment. Are there instructions on the walls explaining what to do in the event of a fire?

Knowing why organisations have policies for health, safety and security, and how these policies protect individuals

When the government introduces laws, care settings and organisations that work with individuals have to respond by producing policies. Policies normally state the overall intentions of an organisation – they state what the organisation will do and what people can expect from the service. Policies will be different in different settings. The health and safety policy in a service that caters for adults will be different from the policy in a service that caters for children – adults will not need to have gates locked for example. Once policies have been written, people then draw up procedures (step-by-step instructions (or rules) you need to follow in order to implement the settings policy).

Policies

Settings will normally have policies on:

» safeguarding children and vulnerable adults

» health and safety – including fire procedures, accidents, safe storage of cleaning materials and medicines

» safe collection of children (who is allowed to take children away from the setting)

» safe storage of valuables and personal belongings

» behaviour

» equal opportunities

» security.

It is important that work settings are safe both for service users and staff. Prevention is better than dealing with an accident or injury.

Work settings have policies so that employers and employees know and understand the rules of working there and keeping the environment safe. They also set out what the law says. Any setting that has more than five employees should display a poster or provide staff with a leaflet showing health and safety law.

Employers can be taken to court if they fail to keep the people in their care safe from harm.

Policies show the aims of an organisation, and the beliefs and values about care that people working share when they work there.

Procedures

Fire safety procedure

It is important that you practise procedures for what to do in the event of an emergency such as a fire. Your fire safety procedure should include unannounced fire drills (where everyone has to leave the building) every six weeks.

In the event of a fire:

» Raise the alarm.

» Collect the register to take to the assembly point.

» Keep calm and walk swiftly.

» Do not attempt to collect personal belongings.

» Evacuate all people from the premises.

» Assemble at the assembly point.

» Do a head count and check people's names against the register.

» Report to the fire warden.

» Do not re-enter the building until permission is given.

FIGURE 5.6 **Symbols for fire evaluation instructions**

TRY THIS

Think about why it is important to practise fire drills every six weeks.

Procedure for dealing with hazardous substances

» Assess the risk – identify whether the substance is dangerous

» Decide what precautions you need to take – for example, where the substance should be kept and how it should be labelled. Should it be locked away in a cupboard?

» If the substance is dangerous, control who has access to it

» Ensure all staff are aware of the procedure and receive training

» Monitor the use of the substance – make sure staff write down when they have used it and sign to say they have locked it away after use

» Prepare plans for emergencies – for example, what to do if someone got hold of the substance by accident.

Procedure for ensuring the security of valuables and property

» Ask service users if they have any valuables they would like to be kept safe – this can be anything they think is important

» Make a list of all valuables that they give to you

» Describe items of jewellery – for example, colour, gold, silver

» Ask the service user to sign for the valuables they have given you and any that they are keeping themselves

» Inform the service user that you are not responsible for any losses

» Lock the valuables in a safe place

» Inform your manager if the service user has kept expensive items or large amounts of money.

ASK

Identify and list the procedures (the step-by-step rules) you need to follow in these situations:

✱ a suspected gas leak

✱ when administering medicines to service users

✱ a missing child

✱ an accident

✱ the late collection of children.

When you have finished investigating and listing the procedures, create a Word file for all your procedures. Insert a header and footer indicating who the procedure was compiled by and the date. Include the page number.

LINKS

> » Ask what staff members have to do if they notice a child is missing.
>
> » Ask what would happen if they did not follow the policies and procedures of the setting.
>
> » Try to find out if service users are aware of these policies and procedures.
>
> » Look to see if there is a health and safety poster or leaflets to give to employees.

Carrying out a basic health and safety risk assessment for a specified setting

Hazards in the care environment

There are hazards everywhere, at work, at home and when you go out. All objects, resources and environments have the potential to be dangerous. A chair can be a hazard if placed in the wrong place or if it is not being used properly. Lots of children have accidents when they swing back on their chairs or accidentally bump into them as they walk past. Every object, every resource and every situation has potential risks. Even water can be a hazard, for example, when it carries the risk of drowning.

There are lots of hazards and potential risks in the workplace. Examples include:

» spillages on the floor – people can slip and hurt themselves

» loose wires – people can electrocute themselves

» faulty equipment – both staff and service users can hurt themselves

- » outings – children can get lost

- » swings – children can run in front of them

- » small objects – children can swallow them

- » worn carpets with frayed or curled-up edges – people may trip on them.

THINK

Make a list of all the possible hazards in your school.

What could be done to stop people having accidents?

If an accident does happen at school, who do you need to report it to?

Risk assessment and the law

Health and safety laws require all settings to undertake **risk assessments**. This basically means that all settings have to identify hazards (possible dangers) and what measures need to be taken (what they need to put in place/do) to ensure everyone's safety.

When doing a risk assessment the workplace setting must:

- » identify the hazard (the danger) and the risk (what might happen)

- » identify how dangerous the situation is and the likelihood of an accident happening

- » identify the controls needed to make sure people are safe (what the setting needs to do)

- » identify who is responsible for making sure people are safe

- » record the date of the risk assessment and sign the document

- » decide when to review the assessment (look at the danger again in the future).

TABLE 5.3 **Example of risk assessment**

Hazard	Risk	Possibility of this happening 1 = low 2 = medium 3 = high	Action that should be taken	Responsibility	Signed and dated	Review
Tea time	Spillages on floor, burns	2	Provide service users with trays, mop spillages immediately, ask service users to drink hot drinks sitting down, do not allow people to walk around with hot drinks	All staff	Sue Cunningham 14 February 2008	September 2008

TEAMWORK

With another learner, carry out a health and safety risk assessment in your school:

✳ Choose **one** hazard and identify **three** risks this could pose to you and to others.

✳ Identify what actions could be taken so that people do not hurt themselves.

Use a table like the one in Table 5.3 to record your findings.

I want to be...

... an environmental health officer

Name: Sam Jones

Age: 30 years

Salary: £30,000 per annum (per year)

Employer: Luton Local Authority

Hours of work: 35 hours per week (7 hours per day)

» Roles and responsibilities (what I do in my job as an environmental health officer):

- I am responsible for making sure that Luton is an environmentally safe place for people to live
- I check restaurants and food premises to ensure that food is fit for people to eat
- I visit schools and colleges to give talks on environmental health issues
- I provide leaflets for people and attend exhibitions
- I check houses and flats to ensure that they are safe for people to live in and the conditions are satisfactory
- I can enforce the law and stop people operating if they are not ensuring the safety of others

» Qualifications:

- A degree in science
- One year of practical training with Luton Council.

» What I like about my job:

Every day is different. I like visiting schools and colleges and talking to young people. I like the flexibility of my job. If I have to work in the evenings checking restaurants I get this time back. This means I can have time off in the day to go shopping and do the things I like.

» The hardest part of my job:

Some of the conditions that I have seen are terrible. In one fast food restaurant I visited there were mice droppings all over the worktops and the bins had not been emptied for a long time. The owner was unaware of the health issues associated with his premises being dirty. The restaurant was used by lots of young people and they were unaware of the risks to their health.

Sam Jones

In the Community

Luton Local →

Environmental Health Officers have today shut down a local fast food restaurant in Luton. Reports received from a variety of sources have indicated that hygiene was exceptionally poor.

When Officers inspected the premises it was found that bins had not been emptied for some time. There were mice droppings on worktops and the owner was using food that had passed its sell-by date.

Environmental Health Officers had been concerned for some time about the number of cases of food poisoning in young adults who used the facilities. It is expected that the owner will be fined and will not be allowed to serve food on these premises again.

Questions

1. How could the owner have stopped the spread of infection?

2. Should the owner be fined and stopped from selling food?

3. Why is it important to have regulations concerning the health of the public?

4. Are some people more vulnerable and more at risk than others?

5. How would you feel if you were served food that was not properly prepared?

6. What foods are high risk in terms of food poisoning?

Assessment Tips

To pass your assessment for this unit you will need to consider carefully all the information in this unit and all the information that has been given to you by your teacher.

Create a Word file for your work and remember to include in your headers and footers your name, candidate number, centre name, centre number, the date and the page number.

FIND OUT

» What are the main causes of infection? Make sure you know about bacterial, fungal and viral infections. You will need to provide one example of each type of infection – for example flu is a virus. You will also need to understand how infections are transmitted – how people catch infections from each other and from the environment.

» How do you protect and support adults and children who are being abused? You will need to understand what employees need to do to ensure that people are not harmed. For example there will be policies and procedures in place so that abuse will be noticed when it is happening. Go back to the section on abuse and identify how staff can help those who may be vulnerable.

» What is the law concerning health and safety and how does the law help to keep people safe? For your assignment you will need to identify three pieces of legislation – make sure you include how the law helps to keep people safe.

» How do the policies implemented by an organisation protect people? For example a policy on who collects children ensures that children do not get taken by strangers.

» How do you carry out a risk assessment in a setting? You will need to make sure you understand the risks associated with certain hazards – for example people can spill hot drinks on themselves, causing burns, or they can spill them on the floor, causing others to slip and hurt themselves.

SUMMARY / SKILLS CHECK

» Main causes of infection

✔ There are three main causes of ill health in humans: micro-organisms (germs), genetic inheritance (what you are born with that you get from your parents) and the environment (things around you that can make you ill, such as poor diet, poor housing, drugs, smoking, alcohol).

✔ The spread of infection can be controlled to some extent by: personal hygiene and always washing your hands, disposing of waste products in a safe way and immunisation against disease – for example, routine vaccination of babies to protect them against diseases such as polio, whooping cough and measles.

» Ways in which vulnerable people can be protected from harm and abuse

✔ Some people intentionally abuse others, or put them at risk of harm. There are different types of abuse, physical, sexual, emotional and neglect. If you suspect abuse or someone tells you they are being abused: listen calmly, believe them, reassure them and do not make judgements. Do not tell the person everything will be OK (it may not be), you must tell them you cannot keep this a secret and you have to inform your supervisor, tell the person in charge and later write down what you were told.

» The protection of vulnerable adults and children and the law

✔ This includes: POVA , Criminal Records Bureau, Children Act 1989, The Children Act 2004, Every Child Matters.

✔ Laws have been passed to safeguard people from harm. The government has identified key areas where people have experienced harm or are at increased risk of injury.

» Why organisations have policies for health, safety and security

✔ Prevention is better than cure.

✔ Organisations have policies for health and safety, child protection, equal opportunities, collection of children, how to administer medicine, what to do if you see an intruder, behaviour and aggression management and risk assessment.

✔ Policies are in place to ensure that law set by government is implemented. Employers can be taken to court if they fail to keep people in their care safe. Policies ensure that staff and service users are clear about the aims of the organisation and know that their environment is safe.

OVERVIEW

This unit has been written to help you learn about people's health and wellbeing. It is important as individuals and as part of the community that we try to eat healthily and look after ourselves. If we do not look after ourselves we may suffer from ill health and need professional care.

Health and wellbeing is also concerned with people's environmental conditions such as housing, access to money, relationships, exposure to crime and pollution.

To a large degree, we are responsible for our own health and wellbeing. However, certain sectors of the community may experience difficulties in following a healthy lifestyle. For example, people who are poor and people who are unable, through disability or disease, to follow a healthy lifestyle, eat a healthy diet or exercise adequately.

The government has tried to promote the health of the nation by advertising healthy lifestyles. We are continually exposed to adverts and programmes promoting the benefits of eating healthy foods such as fruit and vegetables. We are regularly warned about the dangers of alcohol and its effects on our health. In this unit you will learn about how the choices we make in our life affect our health and wellbeing.

When you are looking at this unit, it may help you to use a case study, or the characters from a TV show, to think about their lifestyle choices.

06

Health, Wellbeing and Lifestyle

Skills list

On completion of this unit you should:

» Know how lifestyle choices impact on health and wellbeing

» Understand activities that have a positive and negative effect on health and wellbeing in childhood and throughout life

» Understand the social and economic factors that can have an influence on the health and wellbeing of individuals and communities

» Know the ways in which the health and wellbeing of individuals can be assessed

» Know the normal baseline measurements for health and how these can be measured

» Be able to assess an individual's health, wellbeing and lifestyle.

Job watch

You will need this knowledge if you are considering a career as a:

» doctor
» midwife
» nurse
» health visitor
» early years practitioner
» care worker
» probation officer
» police officer
» teacher
» youth worker
» childminder
» after school worker
» play worker
» health promotion worker
» substance misuse support worker
» drug and alcohol counsellor
» dietician
» school meals supervisor
» school support worker.

FIGURE 6.1 **Obesity leads to ill health**

Knowing how lifestyle choices affect health and wellbeing

What is meant by health and wellbeing

Being healthy involves everything that may affect our physical, social or mental wellbeing. Poor health is not just about being ill – for example, people can be free from infections and disease but still be unhealthy. Health and wellbeing are concerned with the all-round needs of a person.

When we look at health and wellbeing we are looking at lots of different issues, such as:

» housing and where we live

» who we have as friends

» whether we practise safe sex

» whether we are stressed

» what we eat and whether it is good for us

» how much exercise we have

» whether we take drugs

» how much alcohol we drink

» whether we choose to smoke

» how we take care of our personal hygiene

» our emotional health and whether we are happy.

Factors that affect the choices that people make

The question of health, wellbeing and the choices people make is a complex area of study. When we look at this area of study we need to take into consideration the following factors:

» Adults will have some control over whether they eat healthily, smoke, take drugs or drink alcohol, but some individuals will have little control over where they live and how much money they have to spend.

» All people are different and will react to situations differently. Some people who are unemployed still eat healthily and do exercise. We must not make assumptions and expect all people to be the same.

» Certain groups of people are more likely to suffer from some conditions than others. For example, women live longer than men, older people are more likely to experience ill health, people who are unemployed tend to have more illnesses, certain groups of people, such as those who are poor, die earlier than others.

How we are influenced

When we make decisions concerning our health we are influenced by many factors.

» family, peers, friends

» TV, advertising, magazines, other media

» Government initiatives, laws.

How our choices affect our health and wellbeing

The life choices we make can seriously affect our health, either positively or negatively. For example, making sure we have a good diet and enough exercise will keep us fit and healthy. However, poor housing, a poor diet, misuse of drugs, drinking too much alcohol or smoking will have both short-term and longer-term effects on our health. We become more likely to suffer from:

» mental health problems, including depression and self-harm

» behavioural problems, low self-esteem and low achievement

» low or high blood pressure

» heart disease, including heart attacks, and strokes

» breathing problems and asthma

» liver disease and cancer.

We are likely to recover quite quickly from a short-term illness such as a chest infection. Longer-term ill health, however, may lead to lack of social gains such as unemployment and loss of financial rewards.

Drugs and alcohol can affect your health. Design a poster which you can display in your school which tells other young people of the dangers of taking drugs and misusing alcohol.

» Are the service users happy?

» Are there posters on the wall that promote health and wellbeing?

Understanding activities that have a positive and negative effect on health and wellbeing in childhood and throughout life

What is meant by a healthy diet

FIGURE 6.2 Eating fruit and vegetables assists a healthy lifestyle

What you eat and the amount of food you consume can seriously affect your health. People can suffer from malnutrition if they do not eat enough, or if they eat too much of one type of food. It is important to eat food containing the correct nutrients, so that the body:

» has enough energy to function in daily activities

» can grow and develop

» can repair and replace damaged tissues

» generates enough heat to keep itself warm.

Balanced diets

A balanced diet should include foods from the four main food groups:

» carbohydrates

» fats

» vitamins and minerals

» proteins.

TABLE 6.1 **The four main food groups**

Carbohydrates	Fats	Vitamins and minerals	Proteins
bread	butter	fruit	meat
rice	oils	vegetables	fish
beans	cheese	salad	eggs
pasta	nuts		pulses
noodles	meat		
potatoes	fish		
cereals			

If you do not have enough foods from the above groups you can suffer from ill health. For example:

» if you do not have enough **fats** – you will not be able to absorb vitamins

» if you do not have enough **proteins** – you will suffer from lack of energy, failure to grow and develop, and be more prone to infections

» if you do not have enough **carbohydrates** – you will suffer from lack of energy, and be more prone to infections

» if you do not have enough **vitamins and minerals** – you may suffer from poor vision, infections, anaemia, sores in the mouth, and damage to nerves

» if you do not have enough **water** – you will suffer from dehydration, which ultimately leads to death.

JOIN IN

Keep a detailed food diary for the next 24 hours and list all the meals, snacks and drinks you eat or drink.

Discuss your habits with another learner and decide whether your diet is healthy.

Identify whether you have eaten any carbohydrates, fats, vitamins and minerals, and proteins.

Calories and the amount we eat

The amount of food you eat is also important. How much you eat is dependent on:

» whether you are male or female

» whether you are ill

» how much energy you use

» how old you are

» whether you are trying to lose weight

» whether you are trying to gain weight.

FIND OUT

Find out how many calories people of different age groups and sexes need to stay healthy. Make a table to show your findings.

Allergies

Allergies to foods can have serious effects for the individual concerned. Serious allergies can cause death. Some of the most common allergies and intolerances involve reactions to:

» wheat

» milk

» dairy products

» nuts

» fish

» food additives

» chocolate

» caffeine.

Food intolerances can cause stomach upsets, skin rashes, eczema, and changes in behaviour. It is important that you always ask individuals, or their families, if they are allergic to any types of food.

Different diets

There are many different ways of providing a diet that is balanced. Different families will have different cultural and religious backgrounds which influence what they eat.

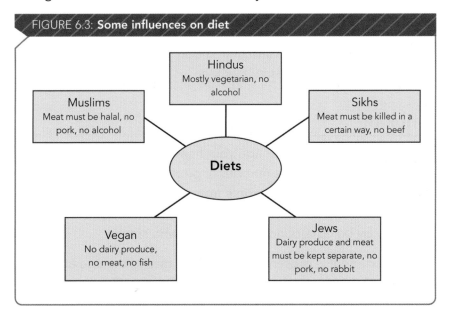

FIGURE 6.3: **Some influences on diet**

Hindus
Mostly vegetarian, no alcohol

Muslims
Meat must be halal, no pork, no alcohol

Sikhs
Meat must be killed in a certain way, no beef

Diets

Vegan
No dairy produce, no meat, no fish

Jews
Dairy produce and meat must be kept separate, no pork, no rabbit

Benefits of a healthy diet

A healthy diet:

» gives your body the energy to do all the activities you want to do

» increases concentration – there is a clear link between diet and intellectual ability and achievement

» helps to fight infection and disease

» helps to protect against long-term illnesses such as heart disease, strokes and cancer

» helps to reduce blood cholesterol

» keeps weight down

» keeps blood pressure down.

Effects of having a poor diet

A poor diet may increase the likelihood of:

» lack of energy and poor concentration, leading to low achievement

» dental decay

» malnutrition, including obesity

» poor resistance to infection

» diabetes

» high blood cholesterol and high blood pressure, leading to heart disease or strokes in later life.

Smoking

Smoking can seriously damage your health. The government in the UK is trying to reduce the number of people who smoke. It has introduced laws stopping people from smoking in the workplace. Individuals can be affected directly by smoking themselves, or indirectly by being around other people who smoke.

The government is presently considering raising the age at which you can buy cigarettes from 16 years to 18 years. If you smoke in your teenage years you are three times more likely to die from cancer than someone who starts smoking in their twenties.

Smoking will also:

» make you smell of cigarette smoke

» cost you a lot – cigarettes are expensive

» give you yellow fingers and teeth

FIGURE 6.4 **Getting the message across**

» cause you to have poor circulation and poor skin tone

» cause you to show early effects of ageing such as wrinkles

» affect your brain – it can make you hyperactive.

Effects of smoking on your health

Smoking can cause:

» death

» cancer

» heart disease

» strokes

» asthma

» breathing difficulties

» shortness of breath

» high blood pressure

» blood clots

» foetal damage (babies can be born small if their mother smokes during pregnancy) and developmental delay.

> **DID YOU KNOW?**
>
> In developed countries, smoking has been identified as responsible for about 2 million deaths a year – almost half of which are in people between 35 and 69 years of age.

Effects of taking drugs on your health

Like smoking, taking drugs can seriously damage your health. Taking drugs alters the chemical balance in your brain. Drugs are particularly harmful to younger people because their brains are still developing. Taking drugs can alter people's behaviour and make them do things they would not normally do.

There are lots of different types of drugs such as cocaine, heroin, cannabis, LSD, magic mushrooms, solvents (glue), amphetamines and skunk weed.

Misusing drugs can have a severe affect on health, for example:

» it may give the individual a false sense of their abilities

» it could cause loss of self-control, making the individual do things they normally would not do

» it may cause headaches and a lack of concentration

- » the individual may have trouble sleeping

- » the individual may become hyperactive, followed by decreased energy levels

- » the individual may become aggressive

- » it may cause mental illnesses such as depression or psychosis

- » a bad reaction or overdose could cause death.

Drug misuse in pregnancy can cause miscarriage. Women who misuse drugs during pregnancy risk damaging their unborn baby and causing developmental delay before and after the baby is born.

Effects of too much alcohol on your health

Alcohol is a type of drug. Occasional drinking is deemed to be safe, and in some cases a glass of red wine is considered beneficial to an individual's health. However, in excess, alcohol can cause:

- » loss of self-control – causing the individual to do things that they normally would not do

- » aggression

- » slow reaction times

- » depression

- » malnutrition – due to lack of nutrients

- » raised blood pressure leading to heart disease and strokes

- » liver damage

- » brain damage

- » death – through an accident when drinking, or eventually due to the long term effects of alcohol on the body.

Drinking alcohol during pregnancy can harm the unborn baby and also cause the baby problems after it is born.

Once you start smoking, drinking alcohol and eating a poor diet, it is hard to stop. It is far better not to start. You need to have will-power and to take responsibility for yourself if you want to be healthy. One way to improve your lifestyle and maintain your health and wellbeing is through exercise.

Exercise

You can exercise in many different ways; for example:

» walking

» swimming

» running

» going to the gym

» playing games such as football, netball, badminton, tennis, etc.

» dancing

» boxing

» walking the dog

» climbing.

FIGURE 6.5 **Exercise should be fun**

Benefits of exercise

Exercise makes you feel good about yourself. It develops confidence and self-esteem. It can also:

» give you more energy

» tone muscles and make you more agile

» help circulation and give you better skin tone

FIND OUT

What is the difference between type 1 and type 2 diabetes? Hint: you can use the NHS Direct website to find out – www.nhsdirect.nhs.uk.

» relieve symptoms of depression and anxiety

» relieve stress and help you to sleep

» stimulate appetite

» develop your immune system so that you are less prone to infection

» decrease your chance of developing conditions such as heart disease, strokes, high blood pressure and type 2 diabetes.

ASK

Look at newspaper and magazine articles, information on the internet, and TV programmes about the increasing number of children suffering from obesity.

Make a list of the reasons why children are becoming more obese in today's society.

With another learner, identify what we can do to make children healthier.

» Look to see if service users take part in some sort of physical activity.

» What kind of food is given to the service users? Is it balanced and healthy?

» Find out if the setting provides different types of food to meet the different cultural and religious needs of the community.

Understanding the social and economic factors that can have an influence on the health and wellbeing of individuals and the community

Social and economic factors can affect people's health and wellbeing. For example, researchers have looked at the statistics for individuals in society and have found a link between poor housing and increased risk of poor health. Research tells us that certain groups who live in certain conditions are more likely to suffer from ill health and premature (early) death than others.

Social factors

Social factors which affect health include:

» poor housing

» living alone (especially in the case of the elderly)

» ethnicity (race)

» whether you live in the country or the city

» individual or group values

» feeling isolated

» whether you are male or female

» criminality.

Economic factors

An individual's economic status has a great effect on their health. Being employed increases self-esteem and confidence, it also gives the individual purchasing power. If you are unemployed you are likely to have a lower self-esteem and may not be able to afford essentials such a housing, healthy food and warm clothing. Poverty has been linked to poor health and disorders such as depression, obesity, heart disease and type 2 diabetes.

FIGURE 6.6
High rise living

What the research tells us

Researchers look at the number of times an event occurs and they link this to social and economic factors. For example, if we look at death statistics for males and females we see that women tend to live longer than men. Overall, women are less likely than men to smoke, take drugs, drink alcohol or get involved in dangerous sports. The research tells us that:

» People from other racial groups do not live as long as white people.

» Afro-Caribbean groups tend to suffer from strokes, but they have low rates of cancer.

» African people tend to have higher blood pressure than other groups.

» White people tend to suffer more from cancer and lung disease.

» Professional workers such as doctors and solicitors live longer than unskilled workers such as cleaners and labourers.

» Poor people die earlier and suffer more from long-term illness than those who are not poor.

» If you live in poor housing you are more likely to suffer from depression.

» If you live in poor housing you have an increased risk of respiratory problems.

» You are more likely to be obese if you are an unskilled worker.

» Working-class women are more likely to suffer from mental health problems than other women.

» People who are working-class do not use the health services as much as professional people.

THINK

Look at what the research tells us. With a fellow learner, discuss why you are more likely to be obese if you are an unskilled worker. Make a list of possible reasons and discuss your findings with the rest of the group.

How can we inform people of the benefits of a healthy diet?

How social and economic factors can influence health

When we look at the social and economic factors that may influence the health of individuals it is essential that we remember that individuals react differently to different situations. Remember the values of the sector – everyone is different. Each person is an individual and we cannot make assumptions about groups of people. However, as we have seen, the way we live does affect our health and in general there are certain factors such as housing, who we live with and whether we are employed or not employed that will affect us all in similar ways. We shall now look at some of these factors.

Housing

If you live in poor housing, such as some high-rise blocks of flats, or houses which are damp and unhygienic, there may be an increased risk of:

» lack of social contact with others

» mental health problems, including depression, stress and anxiety

» poor diet

» infections

» chest complaints, including asthma

» eczema

» substance misuse (as a consequence of depression).

Living alone

People living alone such as the elderly, young people and single parents may not look after themselves properly. There may be an increased risk of:

» lack of social contact with others

» lack of opportunities to go out

» loneliness, depression, anxiety and fear

» lack of exercise

» poor diet – due to not cooking proper meals for themselves

» infection – as a result of poor hygiene

» accidents

» hypothermia – due to lack of heating.

Ethnicity (race)

People from non-white communities are more likely to be unemployed and therefore may lack the financial resources to have a healthy lifestyle. The experience of racism can cause depression, anger and isolation. People of Afro-Caribbean descent may suffer from a disorder called sickle cell disease. This disorder needs specialist treatment and access to specialist units may be difficult.

People of Afro-Caribbean descent also tend to have higher blood pressure than other racial groups and are therefore more likely to suffer from strokes. They tend to die earlier than white people.

However, white people tend to suffer more from cancer and lung disease.

Living in the city or in the country

Living in the city or in a rural community can have an effect on your health. In the city there is an increase risk of pollution and public health problems. In the city you may not know your neighbours and can become isolated.

If you live in a rural community you may have the benefits of fresh air but there may also be high levels of unemployment. People may have limited access to public transport and lack the ability to go out, which can lead to isolation, loneliness, depression and mental health problems.

Individual or group values

We all have different values and believe in different things. Our values can affect how healthy we are. For example:

» Some people believe they should live for the moment and not worry about old age.

» Jehovah's Witnesses believe that people should not share blood and they refuse blood transfusions.

Unemployment

Long-term unemployment can cause depression, mental health problems, including stress and anxiety.

People who are unemployed often have a poor diet and live in poor housing. Poor living conditions may lead to chest and skin complaints and early death.

Financial status

Wealthy people live longer. They are more likely to have healthy diets as they can afford good quality, fresh food. They are also more likely to be able to afford to attend exercise classes and gyms. Wealthy people tend to make more and better use of health services, and they may also have access to private health care.

Poorer people do not use the health services as much. They are more likely to suffer from mental illnesses and physical disorders caused by poor housing, poor diet and lack of exercise. Unskilled workers are more likely to be obese than professional workers.

Criminality

Criminal activity is often linked with mental health problems, including depression and anxiety, and substance misuse. Criminals may take risks that put their health at risk, such as carrying guns and knives or breaking into houses from rooftops and high windows. Once an individual has a criminal record, they may find it harder to find employment.

ASK

Using the Internet, look at one initiative that has been implemented to make the nation healthier – for example, stopping people smoking in the workplace, reducing the number of people who are obese, Jamie Oliver's campaign for healthy eating in schools.

Identify what the initiative was trying to achieve, and the consequences of not implementing this initiative.

Once you have decided on your initiative, use the Internet to find the statistical data on your chosen area – for example, how many people suffer from obesity, what groups of people are more likely to be obese.

Present your data using a bar chart.

LINKS

Knowing the ways in which the health and wellbeing of individuals can be assessed

How individuals are assessed in health and social care settings

Charts

When we work with other individuals it is important that we understand how to assess their health and wellbeing. When children are small we look at how they are developing, as an individual and in comparison to others. If the majority of children start to walk by 18 months then we may become concerned if a child aged 2 years is still crawling.

When children are born, their parents are given a personal health record book which contains charts which show the child's height, weight and head circumference. Each time the child visits a health professional they can see from the chart whether the child is developing normally.

FIND OUT

Ask your carer if they still have your personal health record book.

See if you can find out how heavy and how long you were at birth, 6 months and 12 months.

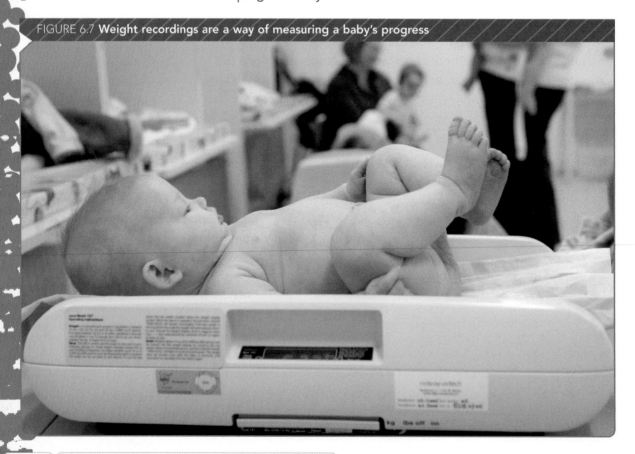

FIGURE 6.7 **Weight recordings are a way of measuring a baby's progress**

ASK

Ask your parent or carer if they still have your personal health record book. If they do not, ask someone who has a small baby. Look at the charts in the book. Are they easy to read? Can you understand them?

Make a list of the individual signs and symptoms that may indicate that all is not well with the health and wellbeing of a baby.

Observations

Observations are used in most health and social care settings to measure and assess the development, health and wellbeing of individuals. Staff will use a variety of methods to observe and record information about an individual's health and wellbeing. For example, charts and checklists may be used to record and monitor information about:

» an individual's breathing, pulse, blood pressure and temperature over a period of time

» height and weight of individuals trying to lose or gain weight

» a baby or young child's developmental progress.

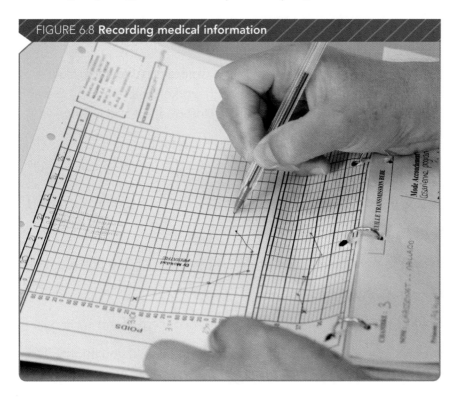
FIGURE 6.8 **Recording medical information**

Observations of service users in health and social care settings are carried out and recorded as a legal requirement. It enables care professionals to share information, with the service user's consent, with other care professionals caring for the same individual. Recording accurate observations to monitor care over a period of time allows care professionals to:

» plan individual care and monitor progress over time

» monitor developmental progress

» give accurate and factual feedback about individual service users

» document patterns of behaviour and any concerns

» monitor people being supported to be independent

» monitor people recently released from custodial sentences

» explore the service user's reaction to care or treatment

» monitor the effectiveness of care or treatment over a period of time.

Case files for individuals are kept that include observations, referral letters, actions by different care agencies and any interviews with the service user, along with their viewpoints. This helps care professionals to see a wider perspective and identify any support that a service user may need.

Interviews

One way of assessing the health and wellbeing of an individual is to interview them. Doctors and health workers will normally use a combination of observations, referral information and interviews.

When interviewing service users it is important to:

» put them at ease

» give them your undivided attention – do not become distracted

» make eye contact with them

» ask the right questions – preferaly use open-ended questions

» listen to them

» allow them time to discuss issues that concern them

» make sure you do not make fun of them, even if you might consider their concerns trivial

» give them time and space to ask questions

» make sure that the service user understands everything you have said

» provide reassurance of confidentiality

» make sure you do not take over the session.

REFLECT

Reflect back to a time when you were interviewed by a health professional. How did you feel? Did you feel comfortable? Did the professional treat you with dignity and respect? Did the professional consult with you and try to establish the main issues? Did you feel that you were given enough information?

Look at the guidelines for interviewing people. Identify why these guidelines are important and how the service user will benefit from this type of approach.

Work in pairs, with one person taking on the role of a GP and the other person pretending to be a service user. Role-play the following scenario:

– The service user is misusing drugs and needs help. The service user goes to her GP for help.

Make notes as you go through this role-play activity. Identify what went well, what did not go so well, and how this could be improved in the future.

» Find out whether staff interview service users, carry out observations, or do a combination of both.

» Visit a health care centre. Ask to see a copy of a personal health record book that they use with children.

» Ask to see a copy of a record sheet used to chart blood pressure, pulse rate and temperature.

Knowing the normal baseline measurements for health and how these can be measured

How health is measured

Body mass index (BMI) is a measure of body fat based on height and weight. Doctors are now using this measurement as a guide to determine obesity. A healthy BMI is anything between 19 and 25. The World Health Organization accepts this definition as an international standard.

FIGURE 6.9 **Height and weight ratios are important throughout life**

ASK

Using the Internet find out how to calculate your own BMI. Identify what category you fit into.

Blood pressure

Most people have their blood pressure measured at some point in their life. Blood pressure provides information about the heart and the blood vessels. A blood pressure reading consists of two values:

» The **systolic pressure** is the maximum pressure in an artery at the moment when the heart is beating and pushing blood around the body.

» The **diastolic pressure** is the lowest pressure in the artery in the moment between beats when the heart is resting.

Both measurements are important. If either is raised it is an indication that something is not right. A person is considered to have high blood pressure if the reading is more than 140/90.

ASK

With another learner find out what tests are done for people who have high cholesterol or diabetes. Identify healthy measurements for cholesterol and blood sugar levels .

Produce a poster for people who may have type 2 diabetes or a high cholesterol level, identifying how they can help themselves.

Being able to assess an individual's health, wellbeing and lifestyle

Assessing the health and wellbeing of individuals

In groups of three, look at the following case studies. Answer the questions that follow each case study.

Mary is 36 years old. She is 1.6m (5 foot 5 inches) in height and her weight is 123kg (19 stone 5 lbs). She is single and lives alone in a one-bedroom flat. She does not have many friends and feels isolated.

Mary visited her doctor because she was constantly thirsty and tired and lacked energy. She could not be bothered to do housework and sits in her dressing gown most days. She is unemployed and finds it difficult to find a job. The doctor observes that Mary lacks enthusiasm and does not concentrate. She is withdrawn and appears to lack confidence.

» Calculate Mary's BMI – is it in the normal range?

» What health problems may Mary be suffering from?

» Using the Internet, research the signs and symptoms of type 2 diabetes, and its treatment.

» What patterns of behaviour must Mary change?

» How will exercise help Mary's depression?

Kenny is 21 and has been a long-term drug user. He is suffering from schizophrenia. He lives with his parents who are both solicitors. His parents are finding Kenny's behaviour difficult. On two occasions Kenny has become violent, and his mother is worried about his and her own safety. Kenny's parents are becoming anxious and fearful when Kenny walks into the room. They are unsure how to handle Kenny and hope one day he will improve.

» What might be the causes of Kenny's schizophrenia?

» What support does Kenny need?

» Will Kenny's schizophrenia cause Kenny's parents to have health and wellbeing problems themselves? If so, what might these be?

» How will the hospital assess Kenny and identify his needs?

I want to be...

... a substance misuse worker

Name: Elaine Roberts

Age: 26 years

Salary: £25,000 per annum (per year)

Employer: Reading District Health Authority

Hours of work: 35 hours per week (7 hours per day)

» Roles and responsibilities (what I do in my job as a substance misuse worker):

– I work in a centre which has been set up to support people who are dependent on drugs and alcohol

– I have a caseload of service users who have been referred to us by the courts

– I make assessments of service users' needs and other factors affecting them

– We provide a drop-in service for people in the community who may be in need of help, advice and guidance

– I help individuals apply for jobs, housing and other services they may need

– I provide counselling services and talk through problems with service users

– We devise plans of action to help service users stay off drugs or alcohol

– We refer service users to other professionals

» Qualifications:

NVQ Level 3 Health and Social Care
BTEC Level 3 Substance Misuse

» What I like about my job:

I like to make a difference to people's lives. I get really excited when people get their lives back and stop using drugs or alcohol. It is really good to see someone change their life around and start to look after themselves.

» The hardest part of my job:

The hardest part of my job is seeing people living in poor conditions. Some people are homeless due to their dependency on drugs and/or alcohol. Some of the service users can also become violent and this can be distressing for me and other individuals. I get really upset when service users die because of their life choices. You are more likely to die early if you abuse alcohol and take drugs. It is really sad to see young people take drugs. They have their whole life ahead of them and they are taking huge chances with their health if they drink too much or take drugs.

❋ Elaine Roberts

In the Community

Living with anorexia →

Natalie is 14 years of age and has anorexia. She lives with her parents in a detached house in the outskirts of the city. Natalie attends school and is doing her exams. She has no friends and she was bullied when she was younger.

Natalie's parents have noticed that Natalie is not eating very much. She has a strange view about her body image. When she looks in the mirror she sees her reflection as fat and ugly. Natalie is obsessed with size zero models. She is very depressed as she feels she will never be as thin as they are.

The doctor has given Natalie anti-depressants, but they are not working. Natalie is getting thinner and thinner. She spends all her time jogging and doing exercises in her room.

Questions

1. What damage is Natalie doing to herself?

2. What will be the effects on Natalie's health in the short-term and long-term?

3. What is the average height and weight for a female aged 14 years?

4. How many calories should a person aged 14 years consume on a daily basis?

5. Why are teenagers concerned about their weight?

6. What are the benefits of doing exercise? Is exercise helping Natalie?

7. How would you help Natalie?

Assessment Tips

This unit is externally assessed. It is important that you revise what you have learnt throughout this unit. Try to take notes and identify key words that will help you remember what you have learnt. Practise with other learners in the group. Devise quizzes and test each other. You will need to make time at home to go through your work.

FIND OUT

>> You will need to make sure you know how lifestyle choices affect health and wellbeing.

>> You will need to understand the different factors that affect health such as diet, smoking, exercise, drugs, alcohol and sexual activity.

>> You will need to identify how your choices affect your health. For example: a poor diet may lead to obesity, high blood pressure, increased risk of heart failure, and diabetes. Unprotected sexual activity increases the risk of infection. Relying on drugs may lead to loss of employment.

>> It is important that you know the advantages and disadvantages of the lifestyle choices that people make. A healthy diet will mean that you are alert, you will have a healthy heart, you will not be overweight, and you will feel good about yourself.

>> It is essential that you remember the positive and negative effects of smoking, diet, exercise, alcohol and drug misuse. You will need to look at the short-term and long-term effects.

>> You will also need to understand the social and economic factors that may affect an individual's health and wellbeing – for example, poor housing, unemployment, poverty, discrimination, living alone, living in a rural or urban environment.

>> You will need to know how social and economic factors can affect people's health. For example: Living in a damp house increases the risk of chest infections. Being poor may mean you have a poor diet. If you are discriminated against and do not have a job you will not have the same choices as other people, and you may suffer from a range of problems such as poor housing, poor diet, and stress, which in turn may lead to substance misuse.

>> It is important that you remember that all people are different and will react to situations differently. Some people who are unemployed still eat healthily and get plenty of exercise. Do not make assumptions and expect all people to be the same.

>> You will need to understand how professionals measure the health of individuals – for example, blood pressure, body mass index (BMI), pulse rate, interviews, observations, height and weight, and individuals' own views on their health.

SUMMARY / SKILLS CHECK

» How lifestyle choices affect health

✓ The life choices that we make can seriously affect our health. Poor diets, taking drugs, drinking too much alcohol, being poor, living alone, living in poor housing and smoking can seriously affect both our short-term and long-term health and wellbeing. Individuals can suffer in a variety of ways; for example, from mental health problems, depression, heart disease and heart attacks, strokes, high blood pressure, low blood pressure, low self-esteem, self-harm, cancer.

» Activities that have a positive and negative effect on health and wellbeing

✓ Activities that will have a positive effect on our health and wellbeing include a well-balanced diet, being happy, exercise and fresh air. Their benefits include making you feel good about yourself, developing confidence and raising self-esteem, relieving stress and decreasing the chances of developing diseases.

✓ Activities that will have negative effect on health and wellbeing include lack of exercise, unhealthy diet, taking drugs, too much alcohol, smoking. The negative effects include depression, raised blood pressure, brain damage, liver damage and malnutrition.

» Social and economic factors that can have an influence on health and wellbeing

✓ Social factors include poor housing, living alone (elderly, single parents with babies and young people), ethnicity (race), whether you live in the country or the city, individual or group values, feeling isolated, whether you are male or female, criminality.

✓ Economic factors include whether you are employed or unemployed, your financial status, poverty.

✓ The negative effects of poor social support or lack of economic power include people not taking care of themselves, poor hygiene, increased risk of infection, poor diet , depression, loneliness, lack of heating, anxiety, fear, lack of social contact with others and increased risk of accidents.

» Ways in which the health and wellbeing of individuals can be assessed

✓ Information about the changes in an individual's health and wellbeing can be recorded and shared with other care professionals. This is usually done by using charts to record observations. Case notes may include charts, care plans, interviews, referral letters, BMI categories, results of tests and so on.

OVERVIEW

Everyone has individual needs and preferences. Our needs and preferences change over time and in different situations. It is important that workers in the different care sectors understand how the individuals in their care prefer to be treated.

All individuals will have basic physical needs – for example, for food, warmth and shelter – but children, young people and adults will also have developmental, social, intellectual and emotional needs.

This unit has been written to help you learn about the needs and preferences that some individuals may have.

Professional care workers must assess the needs of individuals in their care. Once needs have been assessed, individual preferences should be taken into account before planning and implementing a programme of care. Professional care workers may plan care that will be carried out by someone else, quite often a friend or a relative. It is important when reviewing the care given that feedback is gained from everyone who has been involved in caring, including friends and relatives.

This unit has been written to help you learn about some of the needs and preferences that different service users may have. It will also help you to think about planning, implementing and reviewing care. You will also be asked to think about how to collect and record information about individuals' needs and preferences.

07

Meeting Needs

Skills list

On completion of this unit, you should:

» Know the needs and preferences that individuals may have in relation to their health and wellbeing

» Understand how the needs of individuals can be addressed

» Understand the role of the professional in assessing, reviewing and supporting individual needs

» Understand the role of the individual, their families and carers in addressing their needs

» Be able to collect and collate information in relation to an individual's needs.

Knowing the needs and preferences that individuals may have in relation to their health and wellbeing

FIGURE 7.1 **How some London families lived in the early 1920s**

Basic needs

People tend to live longer in today's society. Many years ago the average life span for an individual was around 50 years. Now we often hear of people living until they are 100 years old or more. This is largely due to improved conditions and a better understanding of what makes people healthy. We know for a fact that in order for people to grow, develop and survive it is essential that their basic physical needs are met. In the past people did not always have enough to eat, and they often did not live in hygienic surroundings or have adequate shelter.

JOIN IN

Talk to your grandparents or other elderly people you may know. Ask them how conditions have improved over time. Ask them if they had a bathroom when they were very young. Think about how you would have coped in the past. Discuss your findings with the group.

FIGURE 7.2 **Basic physical needs**

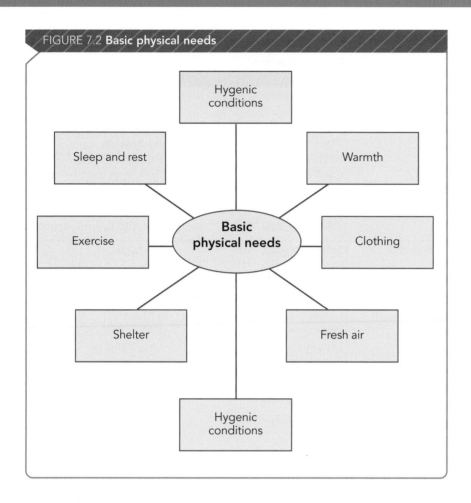

Wellbeing and happiness

How happy people are or how fulfilled they feel in life is not always dependent on just meeting their basic physical needs. As well as basic physical needs it is important to recognise that individuals will also have:

» developmental needs

» social needs

» spiritual needs

» emotional needs

» intellectual needs.

FIGURE 7.3 **Exercise releases natural chemicals that improve mood**

TABLE 7.1 Physical, social and emotional needs

Age and stage	Needs and preferences	
Childhood	Food and water Shelter/housing Hygienic conditions Warmth Bath Clean clothes Shoes Education Protection from harm	Friendships Caring parent Affection Acceptance Exercise Consistent routines Health care Laughter Enjoyment
Adulthood	Food and water Shelter/housing Hygienic conditions Warmth Clothing Employment Leisure Friendships	Marriage Love Exercise Achievement Children Health care Laughter Enjoyment
Old age	Food and water Shelter/housing Hygienic conditions Warmth Clothing Leisure Social contact and friendships Freedom from isolation Economic security (pension) Exercise	Health care Support Affection Acceptance Access to travel Consistent carer Protection from harm Laughter Enjoyment

TEAMWORK

In groups of three, look at the table above and identify for each age group what is a physical need, a social need, an emotional need and an intellectual need (see the example below)

Physical need – food and water

Social need – friendships

Emotional need – affection

Intellectual need – education

For each age group try to add one more physical, social, emotional and intellectual need.

Preferences

How people live their life or like to be cared for varies from individual to individual. Indeed, life would be a bit boring if we all liked the same things. Some people may want to send their children to a same-sex school, while others may decide to educate their children at home. There is no right and wrong way to live your life. Everyone is different and we must respect and celebrate the different opinions of people we come across in our everyday life.

It is important to remember these principles and values in health and social care when meeting the care needs of individuals.

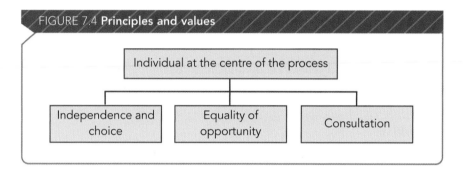

FIGURE 7.4 **Principles and values**

When caring for other individuals it is important:

» to ask individuals what their preferences are – never make assumptions

» to involve service users in developing, implementing and evaluating their own care plan

» to never do for them anything that they can do for themselves

» to provide individuals with a choice and range of services and activities

» to treat everyone fairly

» to understand and identify the individual's developmental stage and needs

» to promote individual rights and beliefs

» to promote diversity and respect differences

» that you do not hold prejudices – for example a common stereotype of the elderly is that they are poor, forgetful, miserable, out of touch, lonely and grumpy. This is not true – all elderly people are different

» not to judge others who have different care practices from your own – for example, some people may wash their hair every day, while others may wash their hair once every two weeks

» to remember there is no such thing as bad food – ill health is caused by too much of one type of food.

Circumstances that can influence the choices we make

In theory we should all be able to make choices in our life that will make us happy. However, life is not always that simple. Factors that can affect the choices we make include:

» where we live

» the services and resources available to us

» unemployment – lack of money

» poverty

» ill health

» mobility

» access to transport

» lack of support from immediate family and friends

» peer pressure

» the influence of the media

» mental health

» lack of knowledge and understanding.

THINK

With a partner, think about all the other circumstances that can affect the choices and preferences that individuals may have. Make a list and share your findings with the rest of the group.

TEAMWORK

In groups of three, design a list of questions that you can use with other learners to find out about their preferred care needs. For example, what do they like to eat? What time do they like to go to bed? Do they have a bath or a shower? Do they have routines that they follow? Do they like hot or cold drinks? How often do they wash their hair?

Identify the different care preferences that learners have in your group.

Discuss with the whole class how you would feel if someone insisted you were cared for in exactly the same way as others – for example, how would you feel if you all had to eat the same food and wear the same clothes?

» Observe different care practices for different individuals.

» Observe whether people from different ethnic backgrounds have different care routines.

» Observe how staff meet the all-round care needs of individuals – are they taking into account the person's physical, social, emotional and intellectual needs?

Understanding how the needs of individuals can be addressed

Care

Care services come in many different shapes and sizes. Children, young people and adults are cared for by their family and friends, in a range of settings, and by a variety of different organisations.

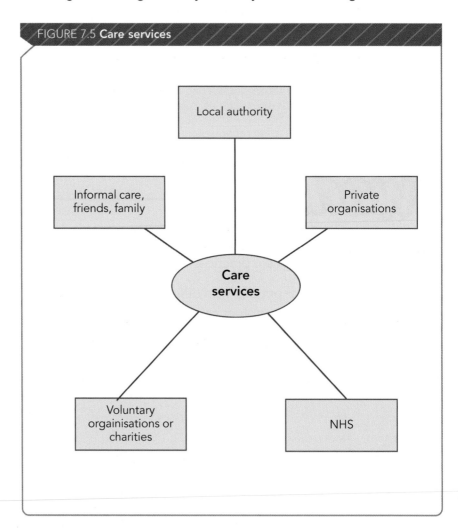

FIGURE 7.5 **Care services**

- Local authority
- Informal care, friends, family
- Private organisations
- Care services
- Voluntary orgainisations or charities
- NHS

How to address the care needs of children

The majority of children are cared for within the family. Their basic needs and preferences are met through care routines provided by their parents and other family members. It is important to remember that all families are different and that other families may be very different from your own.

Children live in a variety of types of family:

» lone parent household – where children live with just one parent

» extended family – where children, parents and other family members such as grandparents live in the same house

» step-parent household – where children live with one biological parent who has a new partner

» nuclear family – where children live with both parents

Some children, due to circumstances outside of their control, may be looked after through other arrangements, such as:

» foster care – a temporary arrangement where a child is placed with another family to be cared for until the child's own circumstances are resolved

» residential care – this is normally provided by the local authority which takes over the parenting responsibility

» adoption – children can be legally adopted and cared for by others who are not related to them biologically. The adoptive parents take on the full responsibility of parenting

» respite care – this type of care is normally provided to help parents who may need a break. For example, some parents who constantly care for children who are severely disabled are able to leave their child with a registered respite carer for a short time.

FIGURE 7.6 **Being loved and cared for is important to children**

TABLE 7.2 Children's needs

Need	Care	Benefits
Food and water	Children should be offered a healthy balanced diet. They should have breakfast, lunch and dinner. Children may also need healthy snacks such as fruit throughout the day. It is important that children have access to water whenever they require it. They should not have to ask for a drink.	Children will grow and develop Gives children energy Repairs damaged tissue Makes children healthy Fights off infection Helps to prevent illness
Fresh air	Children should never be kept indoors for long periods of time. It is important that children have access to fresh air every day. Children like to play outside even when it is raining and snowing.	Gives children energy Stimulates appetite Helps to burn off energy Helps children to relax and sleep Helps to fight off infection Children will be healthy
Clothes and shoes	Clothes should not be too tight. Young children like to play and get dirty and so they need to change often. There is no point in having clothes that are expensive. Clothes should be appropriate for the weather. They should be easy to take off and put on when children go to the toilet. Children should be empowered to choose their own clothes and dress themselves. Children's feet grow quickly. Their feet need to be measured and the correct size shoe should be bought.	Keeps children warm and dry Protects children from the weather Develops sense of self and independence
Stimulation and play	Children learn through play. It is important that children are provided with activities and experiences that they like and enjoy. Activities and experiences should be age- and stage-appropriate (i.e. suited to their level of development). If activities are too easy, children will get bored and lack enthusiasm. If they are too hard, children will switch off and lose confidence.	Supports all-round development – physical, social, emotional, communication and intellectual Develops child's curiosity Develops child's sense of self and self-esteem Children learn about the world around them Children learn skills such as persistence, motivation and determination

TABLE 7.2 **continued...**

Need	Care	Benefits
Affection	Very young children need a key person in their life. They need to feel loved and wanted. They need unconditional acceptance. Children need to be praised and respected for who they are. Through affectionate care routines children learn the skills of parenting and caring which they will need in later life.	Develops child's sense of self and self-esteem Helps children achieve their full potential Develops skills for caring in later life Supports all-round health and wellbeing
Care of teeth	It is important to begin brushing children's teeth as soon as they appear. Brush teeth twice a day. Take children to the dentist from a young age. Avoid sugary drinks and food.	Teeth will be healthy Reduces plaque which causes tooth decay Children will not need fillings
Care of skin and hair	Some children do not like having their hair washed. It is important that you are gentle and protect their eyes. Do not throw water over the child's head. Only wash hair when it has to be done. This can vary depending on the hair type. It is important to seek advice from the child's parents. You should check children's hair regularly for head lice. Children have different types of skin and hair. Some black children will have dry skin and it will need to be moisturised regularly. Children's skin needs to be protected from the sun.	Develops a sense of self-worth and self-esteem Hair brushing helps identify head lice at an early stage and so helps prevent spread of the infection Protecting the skin from the sun helps to prevent skin cancer
Bathing	Young children should never be left in the bath on their own. Bathing should form part of a bedtime routine – bath, teeth and bedtime story. The temperature of the water should always be checked. Use mats that prevent children from slipping. Children like to have toys in the bath – it should be a fun time. Children's skin needs to be dried carefully after bathing.	Children will be clean Helps stop the spread of infection Clean skin is healthy skin Makes child feel relaxed Helps with stress Enjoyment, play time
Rest and sleep	Babies sleep a lot. On average a baby will sleep 16 to 17 hours per day. As children get older they need less sleep. Children under 2 years will need a nap during the day. Under the age of 5, children need at least 12 hours' sleep per night. After this most children will need 8–9 hours' sleep. Children need a bedtime routine which should include a bath, a story and brushing teeth. The bedroom should be warm and comfortable. Some children like to have a night light. It is important to remember that all children are different and some children will need less sleep than others.	Gives the body time to repair damaged tissues Gives the body time to relax Children will be healthy if they have enough sleep – they will be able to fight off infection Children can be miserable, lose concentration and become weepy if they do not have enough rest and sleep

Adults and the elderly

There are more elderly people in today's society. This is partly because people are living longer, but it is also because people now choose to have smaller families than in the past, which means there are fewer children, and the elderly therefore form a bigger proportion of the population. Women tend to live longer than men, so there are a large number of elderly women who need caring for. Although many elderly people live independently, they will still need access to some care services such as chiropody.

Adults and the elderly are cared for in a variety of ways. Some adults and the elderly are cared for by their immediate family, and others are cared for by the state, voluntary groups or private organisations. There are lots of different types of care facilities for adults and the elderly.

Support available to meet the needs and preferences of adults

» **Family members** – family members often take care of their relatives. The relative may live with the family or nearby. There has been an increase in recent years in the number of children who look after their sick or disabled parents.

» **Friends** – many adults and elderly people do not have family members to rely on. Families move away because of their work, and some women choose not to have children. Friends and neighbours often provide the care needed – they will pop in and do the shopping or housework or cook a meal.

» **Care homes** – there are two types of care home: private homes and state-run homes. Care homes are for those who cannot look after themselves and are vulnerable. Residents may need medical care or just looking after.

» **Care in your own home** – local councils send care workers into people's homes. The carer will help with meals, bathing, toileting, dressing and housework.

» **Direct payment support schemes** – money is paid directly to the person who needs care and they can independently pay someone to help them.

» **Nursing agencies** – nurses visit people who need medical care at home. This service is normally provided after someone leaves hospital. Usually this is paid for by the service user.

» **Adult placement schemes** – this is similar to foster care but for adults. Adult placement schemes are normally for those adults with severe learning disabilities, mental health problems or substance misuse problems.

» **Specialist services** – these include groups such as lunch clubs and meals on wheels. Clubs can be for specific groups such as Afro-Caribbean, Asian, etc.

» **Prison service** – the prison service looks after the needs of those who have been imprisoned for breaking the law. It will meet the basic care needs of inmates and try to provide services that will rehabilitate the offender back into the community. Offenders may have additional care needs such as dependency on drugs and alcohol. They may also have educational needs.

» **Hospitals** – hospitals care for people who are sick. Their main concern is the health of the individual. Care can be short-term or long-term depending on the illness.

How to address the care needs of adults and the elderly

Adults and the elderly will have basic needs and preferences similar to those of children. They will need to eat healthily, keep clean and be provided with shelter. They will need to feel valued and unconditionally accepted. However they will also have needs and preferences that are specific to their age group and circumstances. When we work with adults and the elderly it is important to assess the situation and identify the specific circumstances of that person. You must never make assumptions and you should always ask.

Circumstances that may be experienced by the elderly

» Some elderly people over the age of 65 will have large pensions while others will have only a basic state pension.

» Some elderly people will be in good health while others will have a variety of health problems.

» Some elderly people will have more free time to pursue leisure activities while others will lack the resources to participate.

» Many older people live alone and some elderly people may feel isolated.

» Some elderly people have mobility problems.

» Some elderly people continue to work past the age of 65 years.

» Some elderly people may be forgetful, lonely, and unable to cope with independent life.

» Some may be confused or suffer from dementia.

» Some elderly people may be suffering from grief at the loss of a partner.

» Elderly people may be at increased risk of accidents and they may feel frightened.

ASK

Prepare a bowl of cereal. With another learner, practise feeding each other (each person should have a turn at being fed and feeding the other person). The person who is being fed should put their hands behind their back and not help the person who is trying to feed them.

How did it feel to be fed? Did you feel comfortable? Did they put too much food on the spoon? Did they talk to you? How could this experience be more enjoyable?

Discuss this with the rest of the class. Identify what it would feel like if the person tried to force-feed you.

The needs of carers

Those who care for others also need care themselves. It is important to remember that this type of work is stressful and demanding. A majority of care work is done by a family member and often goes unnoticed. Carers in the family often:

» feel isolated and do not have the support of a team

» work 24 hours a day

» perform a variety of tasks on demand

» do not get paid, or receive very little financial reward

» have to escort the family member to appointments with professionals

» do not take holidays

» put the needs of others before their own

» have a limited social life themselves

» feel tired and unsupported and may suffer from stress

» do not have access to training and supervision.

Informal networks

Those who care for others in the family will often need informal support. They will need to discuss issues and concerns with other family members and friends. Informal networks can be a major source of support and assistance. A cup of tea with a neighbour can provide a welcome break.

TEAMWORK

In groups of three, design a poster which outlines the basic care needs of children, young people and adults. Use pictures from magazines and identify the consequences of not meeting these needs.

» Observe the needs and preferences of the elderly and young children.

» What differences are there between the two groups? What similarities are there?

» Observe the behaviour of someone who is tired or in need of a rest.

» Observe whether people have set up informal networks to support and assist each other.

Understanding the role of the professional in assessing, reviewing and supporting individual needs

The process of assessing need in health and social care is clearly laid out. The government has clear rules which determine how money and resources are allocated and spent. There are clear criteria and people are assessed and assigned to one of four categories: critical, substantial, moderate or low.

When professionals are assessing need they will decide what category a person comes under. You are more likely to receive services if your need is assessed as critical or substantial.

The process of care management is a continuous cycle – care is assessed, implemented, reviewed and if necessary adjusted.

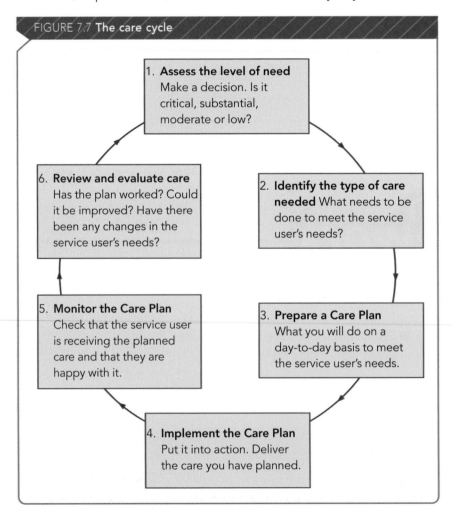

FIGURE 7.7 **The care cycle**

1. **Assess the level of need** Make a decision. Is it critical, substantial, moderate or low?

2. **Identify the type of care needed** What needs to be done to meet the service user's needs?

3. **Prepare a Care Plan** What you will do on a day-to-day basis to meet the service user's needs.

4. **Implement the Care Plan** Put it into action. Deliver the care you have planned.

5. **Monitor the Care Plan** Check that the service user is receiving the planned care and that they are happy with it.

6. **Review and evaluate care** Has the plan worked? Could it be improved? Have there been any changes in the service user's needs?

Who may be consulted and contribute to an assessment of need

- » GP
- » school
- » college
- » nursery
- » carer

- » parent
- » service user
- » friends
- » family members
- » neighbours

- » social worker
- » housing officer
- » benefit agency
- » nursing home staff
- » hospital consultant

THINK

In groups of three, make a list of examples of what you consider to be:

- critical need
- substantial need
- moderate need
- low need

Give reasons for your answers and discuss them with the rest of the class.

The role of the professional in care planning and meeting individual needs

Care professionals have a responsibility to create an individual care plan identifying the needs and preferences of the service user. A care plan is a legal document that looks at the services that will be provided for an individual, and how this will be organised.

Where possible, the service user should be involved in developing their own care plan. When planning and implementing care, the professional carer should:

- » understand the standards of care that are relevant to the setting

- » ensure that information is gathered from the service user and his or her family

- » ensure that information from other sources and other professionals is available to help individuals make choices

- » take a holistic approach – identify all the circumstances that may have an effect on the needs and preferences of an individual

» ensure that the needs of the service user are met and they are provided with choices

» ensure that service users and their families are provided with up-to-date and relevant information

» communicate with carers, and ask for their viewpoints and feedback on the level of service

» update the care plan regularly.

Professional carers should be skilled in asking the right questions, listening to the answers and providing the required information. They should be available to service users when required. Professional carers should be reliable, trustworthy and non-judgemental. When dealing with service users and their families, professional carers should be clear and straight talking (although a sense of humour does help). All conversations and details about care should be kept confidential.

» Ask to see an example of a care plan.

» Talk to people in the setting and ask them about their preferences.

» Think about how you would like to be cared for and how this could be organised in the setting.

Case study – Kay

Kay is 47 years old. She has Parkinson's disease and has difficulty moving about. Just recently her condition has got worse and she regularly falls over. She lives with her children who are aged 20 and 25 years. Both her children have helped with her care in the past but they now both want to go travelling for 12 months. Kay does not have a husband or any other family members nearby.

>> Using the Internet find out what is meant by Parkinson's disease

>> Who should Kay go and see first?

>> What do you think Kay's needs and preferences might be?

>> How can Kay be cared for while her children are away?

Understanding the role of the individual, their family and carers in addressing their needs

How to support individuals with additional needs (disabilities)

>> See the person not the disability

>> Learn about the condition

>> Find out about support and services

>> Make adaptations to the environment if needed

>> Do not make assumptions – ask and find out

>> Avoid labelling and stereotyping

>> Empower people with disabilities – let them make decisions for themselves

>> Build people's self-esteem – look for their strengths not weaknesses

>> Appoint an advocate

>> Challenge discrimination against those who have disabilities

>> Acknowledge that carers may be stressed and have strong feelings

>> Respect the different viewpoints that people may have

>> Liaise with other professionals and work in partnership with others

>> Liaise with family members

>> Ensure that individual care/educational plans are in place.

How to care for and support elderly people

» Visit elderly people regularly

» Like them for who they are and enjoy their company

» Talk to them and comfort them if needed and take their concerns seriously

» Make sure that they are not neglecting themselves and encourage leisure activities

» Check locks and security – put in alarm systems and a security chain on the front door

FIGURE 7.8 **Supporting an individual with additional needs**

» Measure the temperature and make sure the room is kept warm

» Make lists to help them remember things, if needed

» Check hearing aids and glasses

» Monitor medication – check to see if they are taking it correctly

» Check they are eating properly – cook them a healthy, well-balanced meal

» Implement a care plan, if needed

» Seek additional support if needed from social services and/or medical services

» Accompany elderly people to appointments if they need help.

How to support someone who may have been a victim of crime

If someone has witnessed a serious crime or been a victim of crime, you will need to provide support. You should acknowledge that they may be in shock and, if necessary, you should seek medical attention. Stay with the person until they feel safe and comfortable. Listen to them, take them seriously and believe what they are saying.

The police should be informed and you may need to attend the police interview with them. (Later on, you may also need to attend court with them.) If necessary, find out about counselling services for them and involve other care professionals such as victim support services.

FIGURE 7.9 **Crime can have devastating effects**

Being able to collect and collate information in relation to an individual's needs

Case study – Josh

Josh is 11 years old and visually impaired (he is nearly blind). He is very nervous in a new setting and his parents have been over-protective in the past. An educational psychologist has assessed Josh and has recommended that Josh should go to the local school. The educational psychologist has suggested that Josh has above average intelligence and would benefit from attending a local school. Josh has previously attended a special school for those with visual impairment. Josh's parents argue that Josh needs specialist support and should go to a secondary school for the visually impaired. However, the specialist school is some distance away and it would mean that Josh would have to board. Josh is concerned about staying away from home.

1. Who would you consult to gain more information about Josh and his family?

2. What different methods of information gathering could you use to gain information about Josh and his family?

3. What questions would you ask Josh?

4. What questions would you ask Josh's parents?

5. What questions would you ask other professionals?

6. Why is it important to keep this information about Josh confidential?

7. Who else should have access to information about Josh and his family?

8. What school should Josh attend and why?

9. How should records about Josh be stored?

I want to be...

... a care manager for the elderly

Name: Fatima Patel

Age: 38 years

Salary: £25,000 per annum (per year)

Employer: Private sector

Hours of work: 40 hours per week (8 hours per day)

» Roles and responsibilities (what I do in my job as a care manager for the elderly):

- I assess the all-round needs of the elderly people in my care and manage how staff in the setting provide for their care needs
- I manage the budget for the setting
- I am responsible for co-ordinating staff rotas to ensure that we have enough staff on duty
- I am responsible for co-ordinating and assessing the range of services that service users may need
- I work with other professionals such as social services, health care organisations and voluntary groups
- I am responsible for assessing the standard of care provided by the team
- I am responsible for calling team meetings
- I am responsible for domestic and professional staff
- I have to ensure the care home runs properly

» Qualifications:

BTEC National Health and Social Care
NVQ Level 4 Registered Manager (Adults)

» What I like about my job:

I like all the different types of people I come across. I take pride in providing a good service for people who may be vulnerable. I like working with the service users and their families. It is important that you consult with the family at all stages. I like working with my team who are hard-working. We try to enjoy every day and ensure that all residents have a sense of belonging.

» The hardest part of my job:

The hours can be long. I have to cover if staff are off sick. I also find bereavement hard. You can develop close relationships with service users and they can die due to old age and ill health. Family members can become exceptionally distressed. My work can be demanding and stressful at times. I would also like more money and opportunities for promotion.

✷ Fatima Patel

In the Community

Sleeping →

Lucy is 18 months old and lives with her mum and dad in a three-bedroom house. She is lively and happy. She attends a playgroup three times a week to mix with other children. Lucy has difficulties sleeping at night and often falls asleep in the afternoon.

Mobility →

Arthur is 73 years old and lives in a one-bedroom flat on the first floor of a tower block. He has difficulty moving about and lives on his state pension. He does not have any immediate family and his friends have all died.

Learning disability →

Sasha has severe learning disabilities. She lives in a supported unit. Sasha sometimes forgets to wash and the other residents call her names. Sasha appears to wear the same clothes every day.

Criminal behaviour →

Jamie is 14 years old. He has been in trouble with the police for causing trouble and fighting in his local area. Jamie has been taking drugs and drinking with his friends. He has been issued with an ASBO (anti-social behaviour order). His parents find it difficult to cope with his behaviour.

Day centre →

Martin is 48 years old. He attends the day centre drunk and wants a cup of tea. He looks dirty and confused.

Questions

In groups of three, choose one of the above case studies and answer the following questions:

1. What are the basic needs of your chosen individual?

2. What circumstances do we need to take into account for your chosen individual?

3. For your chosen individual, identify the care facilities they may need.

4. How would you support your chosen individual?

5. What other professionals could you call on for help?

Assessment Tips

To pass your assessment for this unit you will need to consider carefully all the information in this chapter and all the information that has been given to you by your teacher.

Create a Word file for your work and remember to include in your headers and footers your name, candidate number, centre name, centre number, the date and the page number.

For this assignment you will need to talk to (interview) a child and an elderly person and make notes on:

» their circumstances and their care needs

» how you could address and meet their care needs

» the roles of three professionals in assessing, reviewing and supporting the needs of these two individuals

» how the individuals can help themselves

» how family, friends and carers can support these two individuals

» how you went about your interviews and how you could improve this in the future.

FIND OUT

» You will need to know about the different needs and preferences that people will have in their lifetime. You will need to identify the different needs that children, adults and the elderly will have.

» You will need to outline the circumstances that can influence individual preferences and identify how you can address individual care needs in a variety of age groups.

» You will need to understand how different professionals across the sectors assess, review and provide support for different individuals in the community.

» You will need to understand how people can help themselves, and how others such as family, friends and carers can support people's care needs.

» You will need to understand how to carry out interviews with people and how to assess their needs. You will need to be able to look back and identify what went well and what went badly. You will need to identify how you could do things better in the future.

SUMMARY / SKILLS CHECK

» Needs and preferences that individuals may have through their life span

✓ Individuals have basic needs for food, water, clothes, shelter and warmth. They also have developmental and psychological needs. People need to be physically and mentally cared for. Needs change with age, children will have different requirements from adults.

✓ Circumstances can influence the choices we make such as where we live, available services and resources, our knowledge and understanding, unemployment – lack of money, poverty, ill health, lack of support from immediate family and friends, peer pressure, media influence, mobility, mental health, developmental delay.

» How care needs are addressed

✓ People receive care from a variety of professionals and organisations. People may be cared for by family members, friends, care homes, in their own home, funded by direct payment, support schemes, carers from nursing agencies, adult placement schemes, foster care, specialist services, prison service, nurseries, after-school clubs.

» Role of the professional in assessing, reviewing and supporting individual needs

✓ Professional carers have a responsibility to assess the category and level of support a person requires. They must prepare care plans to assess the level of care required, implement and monitor care, review, evaluate and adjust care when required.

✓ They must consult with other professionals such as GPs, schools, colleges, nurseries, main carers, parents, benefit agencies, service users, friends and family.

» Role of the individual, their families and carers in addressing needs

✓ When caring for others you must:
- Ask individuals what they like and what are their preferences
- Provide individuals with a choice and range of services and activities
- Promote individual rights and beliefs
- Not judge others who have different care practices from your own
- Make adaptations to the environment if needed.

OVERVIEW

This unit has been written to help you learn about how babies, children, adults and the elderly develop and behave. When you work with young children and adults it is important that you have a basic understanding of how people develop – for example at what age do children begin to walk and when do you expect to get wrinkly skin. It is important that you understand the sequence of development so that you know what is expected and you can help people, if necessary, if they have not reached these expected stages.

In this unit, you will look at how people develop from the cradle to the grave – for example, when do children learn to crawl, walk, run and use a pencil? What is meant by puberty, middle age and the menopause and at what age do people go through these stages?

You will learn to observe children to assess their stage of development – physical, social, emotional and intellectual. Play is an important part of children's development and you will look at what children learn from play activities. You will become skilled at planning and providing play activities for children.

You will also explore the other life events that impact on people's lives as they get older such as starting school, childbirth, marriage, divorce and bereavement.

Growth and Development

Skills list

On completion of this unit, you should:

» Know key physical developments and changes across the lifespan

» Know health and social issues relating to age and ageing

» Be able to assess and individual's stage of development

» Understand what is meant by 'life events' and their impact for individuals and families

» Know the importance of play in the development of children and young people

» Be able to generate ideas and plan development activities for individuals.

Job watch

You will need this knowledge if you are considering a career as a:

» doctor
» midwife
» nurse
» health visitor
» early years practitioner
» care worker
» probation officer
» teacher
» youth worker
» psychologist
» childminder
» after school worker
» play worker
» play therapist
» occupational therapist.

Knowing about key physical developments and changes across the lifespan

Physical development

>> Everyone is different. Except for identical twins who have identical **genes** no two people are the same.

>> Physical development refers to the gradual development of the body and the development of muscles and movements as people go from birth to old age.

>> When we look at physical development we are looking at the skills and abilities that are expected at different stages in life.

>> Physical development refers to the changes people go through in terms of size, weight and body shape.

>> Physical development is concerned with two areas:

- **Gross motor skills** – running, jumping, skipping

- **Fine manipulative skills** – sewing, writing, pointing, picking up small objects

>> Because people are different they will learn to crawl and walk at different ages. All people will walk before they can run. People go through the same sequence of development (they all follow the same pattern) but at different stages and ages.

There are different life stages that people normally pass through – this is sometimes called the maturation process.

FIND OUT

Ask other learners in your group what age they started to learn to crawl and walk. (They may need to ask their parents or carers for help with this.) Compare the differences.

THINK

Think about other terms that are used to describe different age groups – for example, teenagers, the elderly

FIGURE 8.1 **Growing up**

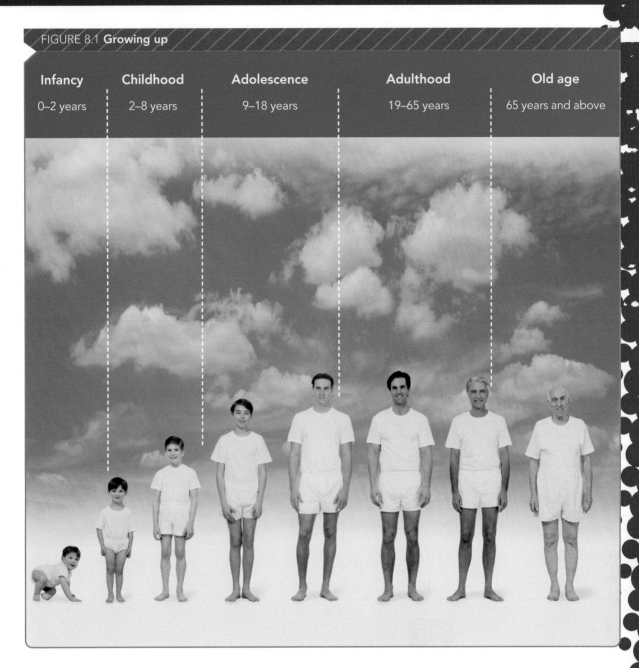

Infancy	Childhood	Adolescence	Adulthood	Old age
0–2 years	2–8 years	9–18 years	19–65 years	65 years and above

Physical development of children aged 0–8 years (infancy and childhood) ↙

ASK

Observe children on the TV, or in the park. What physical activities do they like doing? Make a list of physical activities for children at different ages

TABLE 8.1 Developmental stages

Newborn babies	3 months	6 months
no head control – when you lift the baby up their head will fall backwards lies with head to one side grasps adult fingers turns head to light and noise	lifts head kicks brings hands together pulls to sit begins to reach for objects	sits with support rolls onto stomach reaches out for toy holds arms out to be picked up lifts leg up when lying down has stronger legs
9 months	**12 months**	**15 months**
sits without help for small amount of time can move around floor by rolling	sits without help crawls pulls on furniture to stand walks around furniture can throw toys	walks unsteady movements falls easily pushes wheeled toys
2–3 years	**4–5 years**	**6–8 years**
walks up and down stairs can throw ball kicks ball eagerly can walk on tiptoe jumps can ride a tricycle has bladder control	can walk along a narrow line climbs can run on toes skips can write name	skips using skipping rope can ride a two-wheeled bicycle can swim if taught has good balance can catch a small ball

JOIN IN

Choose one of the following activities.

* Make a mobile for a child aged 3 months. Make a list of all the features it should include. Should it be bright? dull? noisy?

* Make a list of suitable physical activities for people in custodial care.

* Produce a leaflet of physical activities suitable for an elderly person who has had a stroke.

Fine manipulative skills: 0–5 years

Newborn babies

» hands are closed tightly

» grasps adult fingers

» jerky movements

» roots and sucks

3 months

» hands open

» watches own hand

6 months

» can hold objects with whole hand

» smacks objects with whole of hand

» waves and shakes hands

9 months

» stretches out one hand to take objects

» passes objects from one hand to the other

» holds object between finger and thumb

12 months

» picks up small objects such as crumbs

» drops toys on purpose

» points

18 months

» holds pencil in tripod grasp

» can build tower of three blocks

» can put spoon and cup to mouth

2 years

» turns door handles

» holds pencil in preferred hand

» starts to draw

3 years

» can build tower of nine bricks

» begins to dress themselves

» can thread large wooden beads

4 years

» can thread small beads

» has good pencil control

» starts to draw pictures that we can recognise

5 years

» starts to sew

» can thread a big needle

» has good pencil control

FIGURE 8.2 **Fine manipulative skills**

It is important to remember that all children follow the same sequence of development but not at the same age. Every child is different and should be allowed to develop at their own pace.

TEAMWORK

In groups of three, design a poster showing children's physical development from 0 to 8 years. Cut out pictures from magazines or use photographs of yourself when you were younger to demonstrate the physical skills of children aged:

3 months	2 years
6 months	4 years
9 months	6 years
12 months	8 years
18 months	

If you use photographs of other children you know for your poster you must get permission from the child and their parent/carer.

» Ask what practitioners (workers) would do if a child was not developing as expected.

» Find out what adaptations (changes) they would make to the environment for someone who uses a wheelchair.

Knowing about health and social issues related to age and ageing

When people get older they experience further physical changes to their bodies. Teenagers (adolescents) will have learnt all the necessary physical skills needed in life but they will still go through what is known as **puberty**. This is normal and all teenagers will go through this process.

Physical changes in adolescence: 10 to 18 years

The physical changes that occur in puberty are the result of major hormonal activity. Adolescence is a time when rapid and major physical growth occurs. Hormones are released and physical changes begin to happen. For example:

» Both boys and girls become taller, gain weight and grow body hair.

» In girls breasts begin to develop and menstruation (periods) starts and in boys the penis and testicles develop and their voice 'breaks' and gets deeper.

During this period of development teenagers become moody.

» Their friends have a lot of influence over them and they may get into conflict with their parents. They want to become more independent and believe they are grown up.

Teenagers feel they need to belong to a group.

» They tend to sleep more and have an increased appetite.

» They become aware of sexual activities and may be attracted to the opposite sex.

» They start to think about the future and will question what they think is right and wrong.

» They begin to empathise (to show concern for and understand the feelings of others). They worry about their **self-image**. Girls begin to worry about their weight.

Eventually, young adults may want to leave home and live with friends or partners.

DID YOU KNOW?

Self-image is how you see yourself and how others see you.

REFLECT

Reflect on your own self-image. Are you concerned about how you look? Are you worried about being overweight or unattractive to the opposite sex?

Changes and concerns that may be experienced at this time of life include:

» choosing a suitable career

» moving out (leaving home)

» lack of money to do the things you want to do

» increased social activity

» not having any friends

» not being accepted

» finding a girlfriend or boyfriend.

Adulthood: 19–65 years

During early adulthood people do not experience any major physical growth or changes in their body. People are considered to have reached maturity. This means they are fully grown. However between the ages of 40 and 65 years people begin to age. This is known as the ageing process. The effects of ageing can include the following:

» People begin to slow down. They may feel they have less energy and stamina. They cannot run as quickly as they used to.

» Their sight may become poor and they may need glasses.

» At around 50 years of age women go through a major physical change which is called the **menopause** (they stop having periods). The effects of the menopause may cause some women to become moody, tired and depressed; some women may experience hot flushes and night sweats.

» People often put on weight (known as middle-age spread).

» Men may start to lose their hair.

» Some people may begin to forget things.

ASK

Think about why people may put on weight in middle age. Could this be due to lack of exercise? Look around at people you know in this age group. Have they all put on weight?

TABLE 8.2 **Changes and concerns in adulthood**

Positive	Negative
Having money to: e.g. enjoy your social life, buy presents, buy a car or house	Lack of resources and money to: e.g. feed and house yourself, buy clothes, go out with friends
Getting a good job and building a career	Unemployment, not being able to find a suitable job
Finding a partner and enjoying a fulfilling relationship	Insecurities and lack of self-esteem, not being able to find a suitable partner
Becoming independent and leaving home	Isolation – being forced to leave home, moving away from friends and family, lack of support
Having children – maybe through adoption	Not being able to have children or to adopt them
Making new friends through your children – at playgroups, school, etc.	Losing contact with people due to family commitments
Children become independent and leave home	'Empty nest' – not sure of purpose in life without children to care for
Becoming a grandparent	Having to care for your grandchildren when you thought you had become independent again Not having contact with grandchildren – e.g. live to far away, through divorce
Retirement – being able to enjoy leisure pursuits and relationships	Retirement – loss of identity and purpose, lack of money to enjoy life
Being able to care for elderly parents, maybe contributing financially to their care	Having to care for elderly parents, being tied down, feelings of hopelessness and helplessness
	Bereavement – loss of parent or other family member through death

Old age: 65 years plus

From the age of 65 years onwards physical changes take place in the body and in the brain:

» There is a reduction in brain weight and loss of grey matter

» Both physical and mental activity slow down

» Responses are slower

» There is loss of muscle tissue and reduction in lung function

» Skin becomes wrinkly due to loss of elasticity

» People can be unsteady on their feet

» Older people get smaller – as the discs in the spine shrink

» Joints become stiff

DID YOU KNOW?

Frank Cork was 89 years old and suffering with memory loss following a stroke when he gained an Open University degree in Social Sciences in 2007.

The oldest person in the world to gain a Theology PhD (doctorate) from Brunel University in 2004 was 93-year-old Reverend Edgar Dowse.

» Bones are not as strong – many people will need hip and knee replacements

» People suffer loss of hearing and sight

» People experience memory loss

People over 65 years old can be very active and continue to enjoy a fulfilled life. Not all older people have mobility problems, poor eyesight or hearing; nor do they all suffer from dementia. They are still the same people that they were before they turned 65!

It can be easier for people to enjoy their leisure activities, grandchildren and having the time to study when they do not have to go to work. Some people still work for several years after the normal UK retirement age (currently 60 for women and 65 for men).

However, as people get older, particularly those over 80 years of age, they may become lonely as their friends move away or die. This can be especially hard if their partner, husband or wife dies, leaving them on their own. Mobility problems can increase feelings of isolation and depression. Agencies, such as Age Concern and Help the Aged, can arrange for older people to meet together and provide transport to pick them up and take them home again.

The state provides a basic pension and other forms of financial help; for example, with heating bills, free local travel for the over 60s, free or reduced entrance fees for leisure activities, museums and other attractions. Some older people live in poverty as they have nobody to help them claim benefits or they are too proud to take what they consider to be charity.

ASK

Investigate the services that are available in your local area for elderly people. Present your findings in the form of an information leaflet. Photocopy your leaflet and give a copy to the rest of the group.

ASK

Using the Internet, magazines, books and leaflets, research what is meant by an eating disorder such as anorexia or bulimia.

Identify who is most likely to suffer from this condition, and why.

Identify how many people are affected.

Identify support agencies (organisations which can help people who may be suffering from this condition).

When you have finished your research prepare a presentation and present your work to the rest of the group. Try to find out the percentages of young girls/boys who may be suffering from any form of eating disorder. Present your findings in a report with has clear headings and sections.

LINKS

Being able to assess an individual's stage of development

Social development

Milestones is the term which is used to refer to the stages of development that children will go through. Milestones are the key stages of development in a person's life.

Milestones in children's social and emotional development

0–3 months
» cries to get attention

» by 3 months begins to smile

» enjoys the company of its mother

» feeding is a major social occasion

» bonds with mother and immediate carer

6 months
» becomes shy and turns head away from people they do not know

» gives toy to others

» gets upset if mother leaves them

9 months
» smiles in mirror

» is wary of strangers

» plays peekaboo games

12 months
» waves goodbye

» helps with feeding and dressing

» hugs familiar adults

» gets angry if they do not get their own way

» likes to be with a familiar person

18 months
» feeds self

» is happy to play on their own

» becomes clingy

2 years
» knows own name

» knows body parts

» plays alongside other children

» comments on events – 'daddy gone'

» comforts other children if they are crying

» may have tantrums

» likes having their own way

» likes to do things for themselves

3 years
» plays with other children

» starts to share toys

» enjoys helping adults

» can put on clothes that do not have complex fastenings

» likes to have a familiar figure in the background

4 years
» engages in co-operative play

» likes helping

» is becoming more independent

» enjoys simple games

5 years

» knows first name and last name

» comforts others

» enjoys being with other children

» can show off

» their teacher becomes an important person to them

» wants to be liked

6–8 years

» plays games that have rules

» is concerned with justice in games – i.e. is it fair?

» is able to look after others

» can be moody

» likes to be independent

» likes to help others

» wants to be liked by others

» wants to be popular

» may have a best friend

FIGURE 8.3 **Older children like games with set patterns and rules**

Observations

Those who work with children have to observe the development of all children. Practitioners (staff) have to record what they see. Staff observe children for the following reasons:

» it is a legal requirement (i.e. the law says they have to do it)

» to learn about how children are developing

» to assess whether children are behind or advanced in different areas of development

TABLE 8.3 Key development stages

Ages	Intellectual development milestones
0–6 months	Cries to get attention Learns by putting everything in their mouth Learns through the senses – taste, smell, sight
6 months to 1 year	Begins to understand that objects are present even if they cannot see them Tries to copy adults Easily distracted
1–2 years	Can follow simple instructions Talks to self Copies others Can point to body parts Knows name
3 years	Knows colours Beginning to count Can follow instructions that include words such as 'under', 'over'
4 years	Concentration is more developed Can spend a long time at an activity they are enjoying Can write name Enjoys solving problems
5 years	Enjoys solving problems Tells jokes Draws picture of person in detail
7–9 years	Thinking is more complex Begins to understand someone else's point of view Understand concepts such as volume, quantity, weight Beginning to understand right and wrong Beginning to understand the consequences of their actions

» to identify individual needs and if there are any problems with how the child is developing

» to use the information to plan activities in the future

» to provide feedback to parents on their child's progress

» to see how staff are interacting with children

» to see if children are enjoying the activities and experiences provided.

Language development milestones
Communicates through crying, gurgling, cooing Smiles
Sings and hums to self Babbles
Responds to own name Says 'No' Has words such as 'daddy', 'shop', 'car' Starts to put words together incorrectly such as 'daddy go shop'
50 words plus Asks questions Understands more than they can say
Uses complex sentences Enjoys simple jokes Constantly uses terms such as 'why' and 'how' Likes stories
Uses speech correctly 2,500 words plus Beginning to read and write
Can read and write Speech is like adults' speech

FIGURE 8.4 **Two-way communication**

ASK

Make a list of all the physical, emotional, social, intellectual and communication skills that a child aged 3 years should have developed.

Using your list, observe a child aged 3 years whom you know. Identify whether the child has developed all of the skills in your list (this type of observation is known as a checklist).

Look at your findings and summarise what the child is good at, what they cannot do so well and what skills need to be developed.

@work

>> Find out if staff carry out observations of their service users.

>> Find out how they store this information.

>> Find out if they share their observations with relatives.

>> Who else do they share this information with?

Understanding what is meant by life events and their impact on individuals and families

Life events

There are different types of life events that people can experience. These can be:

FIGURE 8.5
Getting married

TABLE 8.4 **Significant life events**	
Planned events, such as:	**Unplanned events, such as:**
starting school	divorce
having children	redundancy
marriage	abuse
starting work	death
retirement	moving house
leaving home	violence

Life events can have a major impact on individuals and their families. It is important to remember that people react differently and that what is planned for one person may be unplanned for another. For example, some children whose parents get divorced may be happy about the situation if they have been constantly exposed to arguments and violence. Some people may be happy to discover they are pregnant, but pregnancy can also be unplanned and unwanted.

When activities are planned, people are normally happy and excited. They are eager to tell others and start organising the event.

However, if events are unplanned they may be seen as stressful. Individuals may react in the following ways:

» They may 'switch off' – for example, children who are concerned about starting school may refuse to learn

» People can become withdrawn, anxious and nervous

» They may respond by being aggressive

» Children may regress in other areas of development – for example, bed wetting

» People can become tearful

» They may display physical signs of distress such as crying or thumb sucking

» People may take little or no interest in what is happening around them

» They may avoid eye contact

» Old people can 'age' (appear to become much older) after their partner dies

» Young people who experience abuse often run away

» Individuals can self-harm (hurt themselves)

» People can start to misuse substances such as drugs and alcohol

» They can lose their self-esteem and confidence

» Individuals can become depressed

Case studies

> **Chantelle** is 14 years old. She lives with her mum and younger brother. She does not see her father and is unsure where he lives. She does not have any other family nearby. Chantelle has become withdrawn and refuses to communicate with her mother. Chantelle has a boyfriend and has just discovered she is pregnant. She wants to keep the baby.

FIGURE 8.6 **Chantelle worries about what will happen to her**

With groups of other learners try to answer the following questions:

>> Is this a planned or an unplanned life event?

>> How might Chantelle react to this life event?

>> How do you think Chantelle's mum will react when she finds out?

>> What impact might this event have on Chantelle in the future?

>> If Chantelle needs help where should she go?

>> What support will Chantelle need?

> **Mary** is 72 years old. She has no children or other immediate family. Mary's husband recently died of a heart attack. Mary does not have many friends and lives alone. She is able to look after herself and is in good health.

With groups of other learners try to answer the following questions:

>> Is this a planned or an unplanned life event?

>> How may Mary react to the loss of her husband?

>> How might Mary feel and what difficulties might she experience?

>> What support may Mary need?

>> If Mary needs help where should she go?

Rashid is 4 years old and is about to start school for the first time. Previously he has been looked after by his mum. Rashid is an only child and has not mixed with other children. Rashid does not speak English.

With groups of other learners try to answer the following questions:

» Is this a planned or an unplanned life event?

» How might Rashid react to this event?

» What behavioural signs might Rashid display?

» How can staff support Rashid and his parents?

» Do all children react in the same way?

ASK

Choose one of the above case studies and produce a leaflet for people who may be experiencing this life event. Identify organisations in your local area who may be able to offer support.

» Ask nursery practitioners if they have a policy for settling in new children.

» Ask how they support children and their families who may be experiencing unexpected life changes.

Knowing about the importance of play in the development of children and young people

FIGURE 8.7 **Playing with sand can help learning and development**

Children learn through play. When children play they are learning the skills necessary for later life. Through play children develop their physical, intellectual, social, emotional and language skills. Play is meant to be fun and enjoyable and it is how the child learns about the world around them.

Children learn through:

» touch

» taste

» smell

» sight

» talking to people

» watching others

» listening.

REFLECT

Think back to when you were a child. What did you enjoy playing with? Who did you like playing with? What skills did you learn from this play experience?

Different types of play

There are lots of different types of play that children can take part in which will help them develop physically, intellectually, socially and emotionally and also help develop their language (communication) skills.

Physical play

Physical play is when a child gets involved in activities that use their gross motor skills (i.e. large muscle movements), such as running, jumping, hopping and skipping.

TABLE 8.5 **Physical play**

Activities and experiences	Development
Tricycles	**Physical**
Skipping ropes	Development of large muscle movements
Slides	Coordination
Swings	Balance
Dens	Fine manipulative skills
Push and pull toys	**Emotional**
Woodwork	Confidence
Rough and tumble play	Self-esteem
Running	Good self-image
Jumping	**Social**
Digging	Sharing
Hopping	How to get on with others
Balls	Co-operation
Throwing	**Intellectual**
Catching	Different parts of the body
Lifting	Distance
Pushing	Speed
Hoops	Height
Balancing	Weight
Walking	Awareness of space
Playing with sand and water	**Language**
Outside play	How to communicate with others
Visits to the park	How to negotiate
	How to ask for help if needed

FIGURE 8.8 **Skipping needs muscles and co-ordination**

Creative play

Creative play is concerned with activities that allow the child to take part in the process of making something, such as pictures, cards and models. It allows the child to use their imagination and display their own ideas and feelings. It is important that children are allowed to get involved in this type of play and that the process is seen as more important than the end product (children can just get involved and do not have to produce something at the end). Children should be allowed to get messy, and it is important to remember that there is no right and wrong way to draw, paint or create something.

FIGURE 8.9
Creative play

TABLE 8.6 **Creative play**

Activities and experiences	Development
Painting Cutting and sticking Model making Junk modelling Book making Colouring Drawing Clay modelling Making cards Cooking Construction – building blocks Games – puzzles, jigsaws Storytelling	**Physical** Development of large muscle movements Co-ordination Hand and eye co-ordination Fine manipulative skills
	Emotional Confidence and self-esteem Achievement Displaying feelings through art work Relaxing Fun
	Social Sharing Working together Co-operation
	Intellectual Imagination Early mark making (writing) Problem solving and making decisions New ideas Counting, measuring, sorting Colours, shapes, size
	Language How to communicate with others How to negotiate How to ask for help if needed New vocabulary (new words) Listening

Imaginative play

Imaginative play involves pretend play. It involves pretending to be someone else. It gives children the opportunity to practise and explore their own feelings and the feelings of others. They will learn and practise skills they have seen and heard.

TABLE 8.7 Imaginative play

Activities and experiences	Development
Painting Dressing up Playing shop Role play Dens Bags Shoes Clothes from other cultures such as saris Puppets Books Dolls Prams Miniature cups and saucers Household items Fantasy play Music Home play areas	**Physical** Development of large muscle movements Co-ordination Hand and eye co-ordination Fine manipulative skills
	Emotional Confidence and self-esteem Displaying feelings through pretending Relaxing Fun
	Social Sharing Working together Co-operation Negotiation Allocation of roles
	Intellectual Imagination Problem solving and making decisions New ideas Counting, measuring, sorting Colours, shapes, size Remembering things they have seen – memory
	Language How to communicate with others How to negotiate How to ask for help if needed New vocabulary (new words) Listening

FIGURE 8.10 **Dressing up and imaginative play**

Other play experiences

TEAMWORK

In teams of three, prepare a presentation for the rest of the group on a chosen area of play such as construction, books and story telling, or music and movement. Your presentation should include the benefits of this type of play. Each person should contribute and you will need to make notes on what you did personally.

Different developmental stages of play

All children go through stages of play. To begin with, babies play all by themselves and are unaware of others around them. Older children play co-operatively and each one will have a role – a part to play in the game. There are special terms used to describe the different stages of play:

TABLE 8.8 Developmental stages of play	
Solitary play: babies	**Parallel play: 1–2 years**
Play completely by themselves, unaware of others around them. No understanding of sharing or playing with another.	Children may play alongside each other. Both do the same activity, but they will not engage with each other. Spend time watching one another but will not play together.
Cooperative play: 3–4 years	**Friendships: 4 years plus**
Begin to play together. Take on different roles and follow the rules of the game in a coordinated way.	Begin to have friends and preferences about who they like. Some children will have a best friend, others will have lots of friends.

In pairs, choose one of the following age groups:

✱ a baby aged 9 months

✱ a 2 year old

✱ a 3 year old

✱ a 5 year old

✱ a 9 year old

Make a shopping list of toys and/or experiences that could be given to a child in the chosen age range. Identify what skills these experiences or toys will develop.

>> Observe children playing. What skills are they developing?

>> How do staff is set out play experiences?

>> What do children like doing?

>> What adaptations do staff make for children having difficulties playing?

Being able to generate ideas and plan development activities for individuals

When you provide activities for children it is important that you plan beforehand. There are lots of issues to think about. You will need to consider many health and safety requirments including the age of the children and whether the activity is suitable for that age group and what development you want to encourage (for example, if a child needs to develop physically, you may want to provide an activity that will help with this, such as outside play). You will need to make observations of the children and what they like doing.

You will also need to think about the role of the adult, **anti-bias practice** and the resources that you will need to collect together for your chosen activity.

Health and safety

When planning activities you will need to consider the safety of the children. You will need to take the following things into consideration:

» Are the materials toxic (poisonous)?

» Are any of the objects dangerous (for example, could babies choke on the small pieces)?

» Are the activities dangerous (for example, could children fall off and hurt themselves)? Remember, children should not be allowed to climb in dressing-up clothes.

» Are the toys kept clean and washed regularly?

» Do toys have the safety kitemark?

» Are materials safe to use? (Make sure you do not use empty toilet rolls for junk modelling)

» Can children wash their hands before and after the activity?

» When cooking with children do they have their own utensils?

» Are there any loose wires or other things that children might trip over?

» Is there enough space?

» Have you carried out a **risk assessment** ?

Developmentally appropriate activities

It is important that you consider the age of the child when planning activities. Children will switch off if an activity is too hard and they will become bored if it is too easy.

TABLE 8.9 **Age-appropriate activities**

Babies	1–2 years	2–3 years
mobiles	pots and pans	jigsaws
rattles	shoes	music and movement
teddies	bags	dressing up clothes
bath toys	toys to push and pull	painting
outings	boxes	sand and water
	books	home area
	finger rhymes	climbing
	outings	bicycles
		prams
		dolls
		cooking
		washing up
		bath toys
		toys to ride on
		large Lego
		outings

3–4 years	5–6 years	6–8 years
cutting and sticking	sewing	sewing
clay modelling	football	computers
junk modelling	skipping	skipping
matching games	musical instruments	team games
jigsaws	PE	books
pretend play	table-top games	bicycles
dens	books	fine detailed art work
books and story telling	jokes	projects
writing and mark making games	model making	comics
Lego	cooking	outings
bricks	outings	swimming
construction	swimming	clubs
music and movement		
cooking		
outings		

Role of the adult

Adults have key roles and responsibilities when they provide play activities for children. These include:

» observing children to find out what they like to do

» making sure the activity is fun and is not boring

» making sure the activity is age- and stage-appropriate

» collecting the resources

» setting up the activity

» informing parents about planned activities

» introducing new language and vocabulary

» letting the children do the activity – not taking over

» praising the child for their efforts

» ensuring that everyone has a turn

» adapting resources for children who may have additional needs

» making sure children are safe.

Anti-bias practice

Ask children what they enjoy doing and try to match your activities to their needs. Resources should reflect the children's different backgrounds. You should provide dressing-up clothes from different ethnic groups, such as saris and kalwar shameez. People from different cultures should be shown positively in books and posters. Musical instruments and music from around the world should be available. Children should be given the opportunity to taste foods from different cultures.

FIGURE 8.11 **Children need a variety of play opportunities**

Boys and girls should be encouraged to join in the same games and play with the same toys. For example, you should encourage boys to play with dolls and girls to play football or play with cars. You will need to adapt resources so that any children with a disability can play with the other children.

Everyone is different and individual. You should praise children and make them feel good about themselves. It is important to give each child an equal amount of your time and help children who are having difficulty playing or settling in.

TEAMWORK

In groups of three, look at the following Activity Plan and answer the questions in each section.

Activity Plan
Sand activity for children aged 3 years

Learning (aim of the activity)
Identify what the children will learn by doing this activity – what skills will they develop?

Implementation (how you will do the activity)
Identify what resources (equipment) you will need

How would you set up this activity?

How would you approach this activity and get children interested?

Role of the adult
Identify what health and safety issues you need to consider

What questions would you ask the children when they were doing this activity?

What would you do if children started to throw sand at each other?

What would you do if a parent complained about their child getting sand in their hair?

How would you encourage a shy child to get involved?

What adaptations would you make for a child who uses a wheelchair?

Anti-bias practice
How will you adapt your activity for children who may have disabilities?

How will you include children who come from different backgrounds?

» How do staff meet the needs of those from different backgrounds?

» How do they meet the needs of children with disabilities or other additional needs?

» How do they communicate with people who do not speak English?

In the Community

Wheel Barrows →

Wheel Barrows is a nursery for children aged 3–5 years. Just recently parents have been complaining that their children are just playing. They are concerned that their children are not learning. The workers at Wheel Barrows believe that children learn through play and this gives them the skills necessary for later life. They believe that children's play should be freely chosen. One parent has complained and said she does not want her son playing with dolls.

Questions

1. What do children learn through play?

2. What activities are suitable for children aged 3–5 years?

3. What are the benefits of boys playing with dolls?

4. What is meant by anti-discriminatory practice (equal opportunities)?

When you have answered these questions, write a letter that could be sent to parents explaining what children learn through play.

I want

dale

Assessment Tips

To pass your assessment for this unit you will need to consider carefully all the information in this chapter and all the information that has been given to you by your teacher.

Create a Word file for your work and remember to include in your headers and footers your name, candidate number, centre name, centre number, the date and the page number.

FIND OUT

» You will need to know about the different physical development stages from birth to old age. You will need to identify the key milestones in development. Look at the development chart at the beginning of this unit and pick out the key stages that people go through. Remember to look at both gross motor and fine motor skills.

» You will need to know about the social and health issues related to ageing – for example, puberty, the menopause, and the key characteristics of these stages. You must ensure that you include three characteristics in total.

» You will need to carry out an observation on an individual's development. The best way to do this is using a checklist. Tick off what the person can and cannot do. You will need to make comments about their development and whether the individual is behind, on track or advanced in their development for their age group.

» You will need to look at major life events such as marriage, divorce, starting school. You will need to explain what these terms mean and how they can affect individuals differently.

» You will need to identify three types of play and you will need to know how each type of play helps children develop physically, socially and emotionally. A suggested way to present this information is in the form of a chart.

» You will need to identify three activities you could do with children. For two of your chosen activities discuss what resources you would need, how you would set the activity up, how you would implement it with children, and what your role would be (i.e. what you would do).

SUMMARY / SKILLS CHECK

» Physical developments and changes across the lifespan

✔ Physical development refers to the gradual development and use of muscles and movements from birth to old age. It is the gross motor skills and fine manipulative skills expected at different stages in life. It is also growth in height and weight and changes such as puberty, menopause and ageing that all people experience.

✔ All children follow the same sequence of development, but not at the same age. Some develop skills quickly, others will take their time. Everyone is individual and different and should be allowed to develop at their own pace.

» Issues relating to age and ageing

✔ Physical changes in adolescence (10 to 18 years) include: increase in body hair, becoming taller and gaining weight, girls develop breasts and their periods (menstruation) start, boys penises and testicles grow larger and their voices 'break' – get lower and deeper.

✔ In early adulthood there is not much physical growth or change. Between the age of 40 and 65 years there are increased signs of ageing. People begin to slow down, eyesight may become poor, needing glasses (spectacles) to see clearly. There may be a decrease in energy and stamina. At around 50 years of age, women go through a major physical change – the menopause – periods stop and they may experience symptoms such as hot flushes.

» Development in other areas

✔ Milestones is the term used to refer to intellectual, language, social and emotional development stages.

» Life events

✔ Events that impact on individuals and their families such as divorce, death, moving house, getting married, having a baby or starting school. It is important to remember that people react differently to these events – what is planned and expected for one person may be unplanned and unwelcome for another.

✔ Unplanned events can be stressful. Individuals may react by switching off, refusing to learn or by becoming withdrawn, aggressive, anxious or nervous. Physical signs of distress include crying, thumb sucking, lack of interest in what is happening around them and avoiding eye contact. Old people can appear to be older after their partner dies.

Useful websites

www.nhsdirect.nhs.uk
NHS Direct provides information and advice about health, illnesses and health services. It offers a 24-hour telephone service with advice from fully-trained health care professionals. More than two million people a month use this service.

www.hpa.org.uk
The Health Protection Agency provides support and advice to the NHS, local authorities, emergency services and many other health-related organisations. Its website has information about infectious diseases, chemicals, poisons and radiation.

www.bupa.co.uk
Bupa is a global health and care organisation. The website gives information about health insurance as well as other services Bupa provides, including care homes, childcare and travel insurance.

www.workplacelaw.net
A website for managers and employers, specialising in health & safety, premises management and employment law.

www.cancer.org.uk
Cancer Research UK funds cancer research in the UK. Its website offers information about specific cancers and clinical trials. It includes questions that people can ask their doctors, but does not give information about treatments.

www.cancer.org
The American Cancer Society website gives information to sufferers about choices they can make and has sections for friends and family to help them work through the difficult times.

www.ash.org.uk
Action on Smoking and Health is a charity that campaigns for national and international changes to eliminate the harmful effects of smoking.

www.talktofrank.com
Frank is a website set up for young people to inform them about the affects of drugs and how to deal with friends that you suspect may be taking drugs.

www.drugscope.org.uk
Drugscope is the UK's leading independent centre of expertise on drugs. Their aim is to inform policy development and reduce drug-related risk. The website provides information about drugs, promotes effective responses to drug-taking and encourages informed debate.

www.kidscape.org.uk
Kidscape is a charity that works to prevent bullying and child abuse. The website gives details to children, parents and professionals about what to do if bullying does occur.

www.nspcc.org.uk
The National Society for Prevention of Cruelty to Children is a charity that works to protect children from harm. Its website has information about all current campaigns and includes details about Childline.

www.everychildmatters.gov.uk
Every Child Matters is a government plan to give children the support they need to be healthy, safe and enjoy life. The website contains details of how this will be achieved in partnership with local authorities and children's trusts.

Glossary

abuse improper treatment or usage of a defenceless individual, such as a child or elderly person, by someone more powerful. May be in the form of physical, sexual or mental ill treatment, or may be through deliberate neglect of the individual's needs.

additional needs individual needs caused by ill health or disability. For example, someone who is deaf may need a hearing aid to communicate with other individuals.

adoption when care for a child is permanently assigned to a parent or parents who may not be biologically related to the child.

advocacy speaking on behalf of someone not able to speak for themselves; for example, an unconscious person, someone with severe mental health issues or someone with dementia.

anti-bias practice another term for equality of opportunity.

body language non-verbal communication: gestures, expression and poses by which individuals communicate with each other without words.

body mass index (BMI) a formula used to express body weight in relation to height. It is calculated by dividing an individual's weight in kilograms by the square of their height in metres.

Braille a form of communication used by people with impaired vision which is a system of raised dots that can be read with the fingers.

British Sign Language a systems of signs and hand movements developed by deaf people to communicate with others.

care homes provide residential care for the elderly, those with additional needs or children.

care plan an assessment of an individual's needs, with details of the services that will be provided and any risks to the individual if these services are not provided. Frequent review and reassessment is made to ensure that the care implemented is working and, if not, adjustment will be made to the plan.

confidentiality the term used to refer to the safekeeping and protection of information about people who come into contact with care settings.

counselling a confidential process between an individual and a care provider in which the individual is helped to deal with personal problems or conflict with others.

disability a physical or mental condition that limits an individual's ability to perform certain actions or functions normally.

discrimination treating someone more or less favourably than others on the basis of their age, gender, race, religion or disability.

diversity a term that refers to the idea that everyone is different, with different ideas and different ways of doing things.

empowerment allowing an individual the personal power to participate in decisions about their care.

ethics the principles used by individuals to decide what is right or wrong, good or bad.

ethnic group a group of people who share common beliefs, customs and traditions.

equality having access to the same rights, services and treatments as other individuals regardless of age, gender, race, religion or disability.

equality of opportunity having equal access and chances to achieve the same things as other individuals in society.

fine manipulative skills physical co-ordination abilities such as sewing, writing, pointing or picking up small objects.

first aid emergency care and treatment given to a sick or injured person to prevent further injury or death until more advanced medical care is available.

foster care a temporary arrangement when a child is placed with another family to be cared for until they can return to their own family, or they are adopted.

gender being either male or female.

germ a micro-organism such as a bacterium, fungus or virus that enters the body and causes an infection.

gross motor skills physical abilities, such as running, jumping and skipping.

harassment any behaviour that is unwanted and offensive that makes another person feel uncomfortable, embarrassed or frightened.

homophobia a dislike or fear of people who are homosexual.

hygiene keeping objects and their surroundings clean and free from germs so as to avoid infection.

immunisation a way of protecting an individual against some infectious diseases, usually by injecting a small amount of the modified germ that causes the illness. In the UK, parents are encouraged to have their children immunised against common childhood illnesses such as mumps, measles and diphtheria through a programme of vaccinations that start in infancy.

inclusion the policy of including everyone in all activities regardless of age, gender, race, religion or disability.

key worker the member of a care team responsible for making sure that other care professionals involved in an individual's treatment and care know about any plans and decisions that have been made.

learning agreements (contracts) a contract between a learner and their teacher that states what behaviour is expected from the learner and what guidance and facilities the teacher will provide.

life events key events that impact on individuals and their families; for example, marriage, divorce, pregnancy, childbirth, starting school, moving house, redundancy and death.

Makaton a form of communication used by people who are deaf that uses some speech, body language and signs.

menopause the time, usually around 50 years of age, when women stop being fertile and their periods stop. This is a time of hormonal change that can cause hot sweats, change in body fat distribution and mental changes such as depression.

milestones the key stages of development in a person's life.

National Strategic Partnership Forum an organisation that co-ordinates the partnership arrangements of the different care sectors, and helps them work together effectively.

non-verbal communication another term for body language: includes tone of voice, facial expressions, hand gestures and body postures.

organisations groups that work together in structured ways to provide a service. These include statutory organisations, voluntary organisations and private organisations.

partnership networking and collaborative working with people from a variety of sectors; sharing information and co-ordinating services to meet the needs of individuals and their families.

prejudice a preconceived opinion against or in favour of an individual or a group of people. It normally refers to pre-judging people without knowing them (jumping to conclusions).

principles the rules (ethics) by which an individual conducts their life and makes decisions.

private organisations commercial organisations whose services are paid for directly by the service user or through insurance schemes.

puberty   a time of rapid and major physical growth between the ages of 10 and 18 when hormones are released and physical changes begin to happen. For example, body hair grows, boys and girls become taller and gain weight, girls develop breasts and start to menstruate (have periods); in boys the penis and testicles develop and their voice 'breaks' (gets deeper).

racism   believing that a racial group is inferior and has less rights than other racial groups, and treating them less favourably.

reflective practice   a process whereby a carer looks back (reflects) at the care given to an individual and identifies important things that they have learned, in order to improve their future practice.

residential care   care usually provided by a local authority for individuals who would otherwise not be able to care for themselves; for example, children, individuals with severe mental health problems and elderly individuals who are physically or mentally infirm.

respite care   short-term care provided to give carers a break from their responsibilities.

responsibilities   usually come with rights and are the duties of an individual to carry out certain actions demanded by events. For example, it is the right of individuals in the UK to receive state education. However, it is the responsibility of the individual to attend lessons and learn about a subject.

rights   powers or privileges granted to an individual by custom or law. For example, it is an individual's right to be treated by care workers with respect and dignity.

risk assessment   identifying hazards (possible dangers) and what should be done to ensure everyone's safety.

self-image   how an individual sees themselves and how they think others see them.

service user   any individual who uses care services, often referred to as a client or patient.

sexism   treating someone more or less favourably because of their gender; believing that one gender is superior.

sign   something that you can observe about an individual that shows they are suffering from an illness or infection. For example, a runny nose may be a sign that someone has a cold or allergy.

statutory organisations   organisations funded by the state through taxes; includes social work, housing and day centres.

stereotype   a fixed idea about a group of people; for example, 'all girls cry', 'all young people take drugs'.

symptom   something an individual complains about when they feel unwell; for example, a headache or chest pain.

values   the beliefs, ideals and customs of a social group; the principles and standards about what is important or valuable to that group.

voluntary organisations   groups that are largely self-funded, but may have some government funding. These include charities such as the NSPCC and the Alzheimer's Society. Some or all of the people who work for them will be volunteers who provide their services for free.

Index